DANCING
IN THE
MOONLIGHT

Ronnie Barker

·············(·············

DANCING IN THE MOONLIGHT

Early Years on the Stage

Coronet Books
Hodder and Stoughton

First published in Great Britain in 1993 by
Hodder and Stoughton
a division of Hodder Headline PLC

Coronet edition 1994

10 9 8 7 6 5 4 3 2 1

British Library Cataloguing in Publication Data

Barker, Ronnie
Dancing in the Moonlight: Early Years
on the Stage
I. Title
792.092

ISBN 0-340-60977-X

Printed and bound in Great Britain by
Cox and Wyman Ltd, Reading, Berks.

Photoset by Rowland Phototypesetting Ltd,
Bury St Edmunds, Suffolk.

Hodder and Stoughton Ltd
A Division of Hodder Headline PLC
338 Euston Road
London NW1 3BH

This book is dedicated to the three wise men
who directed my career:

Horace Wentworth, Glenn Melvyn and Frank Shelley.

Without men like these, there would be no Theatre.
God bless them all.

Author's Note

This book concerns my years in repertory theatres, 1948–1954.

Some of the names have been changed, and it is for the most part accurate in detail, but I have very little documentation of this period, and have relied on memories patched together.

This being so, in among the patchwork one is bound to encounter a little embroidery.

DANCING
IN THE
MOONLIGHT

······· (·······

1

'I can offer you two pounds ten a week – you can start tonight.'

The voice belonged to a middle-aged man with heavy eyebrows and a gammy leg called Horace Wentworth. Or rather, the man's name was Horace Wentworth; I don't know what his leg was called. I had just read to him a page of script in six different accents, which I suppose for a nineteen-year-old bank clerk who had lived all his life in Oxford wasn't a bad effort. But I had been brought up on the wireless and comedy programmes such as *ITMA*, *Up the Pole* and *Stand Easy*. I had a very good ear for accents, and also a musical ear. I've never known which ear was which, but they are both large and stand out like open taxi doors.

'Well?' said Mr Wentworth after he had allowed a suitable time to elapse for me to recover from my dumbstruck delight at his offer. 'What do you say?'

'Oh, yes, thank you, but please, I can't start tonight, I have to give a week's notice at the bank.'

'Well, next Monday then. Now, if you will excuse me, it's ten o'clock, time I started rehearsal. Come on, let's have you!' he roared suddenly. I reacted violently and stepped backward onto an ashtray containing his briar pipe, before realising that the bellow was not directed at me, but at the hidden group of actors lurking in the wings of the little theatre. They duly wandered onto the stage, peering down over the footlights into the auditorium. There we were, Mr Wentworth seated in the fifth row of the stalls, his gammy leg sprawled out across the aisle, and I, standing nervously on his pipe.

'Morning, Horace,' they chorused.

'Morning all, where's Badger, my script's got the first three pages missing.' A lanky blond-haired lad appeared, thrusting aside the aged curtain. The resulting dust-cloud caused Doreen, the leading character actress, to begin a paroxysm of coughing which she only managed to control by lighting up a Capstan Full Strength and taking a deep drag on it.

'Sorry, Horace,' called the lad in unmistakably Etonian tones, 'I think you've got my copy.' He clattered down the three steps at the side of the stage and swapped his dog-eared script for that of the Producer.

'Badger, this is Ronald Barker. He'll be starting with us next week as ASM. This is Patrick Flynn, known for some reason as Badger. Don't ask me why.'

'Splendid,' said Badger, nodding in an affable, daft sort of way. 'See you next week then. Shall we start then, Horace?' Without waiting for an answer, he was gone.

Stepping gingerly out of the ashtray, I too made myself scarce. The auditorium doors clanged shut behind me, and I was once more in the real world.

'Quiet, for Christ's sake,' bellowed Horace. 'Close those bloody doors quietly!' But I, the bank clerk, was not yet under his jurisdiction. I was safe from his wrath, until Monday next . . .

I stepped out into the sunny ramshackle square of Aylesbury's market-place, and floated on a cloud of euphoria to the bus-stop. My dreams had come true. I was to be a professional actor!

The billboard outside the theatre said, 'The famous Manchester Repertory Company' and it did not occur to me to question the fact that it now found itself in Aylesbury, Bucks. The only thing that mattered was that I was now part of it. Oh joy, oh rapture!

I gave the bus-conductor a seraphic smile, and she gave me a two-and-threepenny one to Oxford and threepence change. The sight of this youth with too much hair and a sickly grin obviously disturbed her, for her face hardened and she muttered, as if to me alone, 'Hold *very* tight, please,' and tweaked the cord above her head. The bus lurched forward and I collapsed onto the bench next to the sign which said *Accumulators must not be placed on seats* and opposite the sign which said *No spitting*. Intending, as I did, to do neither of these things, my sense of freedom knew no bounds. My heart was as light as a feather. The aura of happiness surrounding me was such that I had to take the conductress's advice and hold *very* tight, to prevent myself bursting into song, or as my younger sister called it, noise. I longed to burst into noise. An actor! Me! I contented myself with quietly humming snatches of an old folk-noise under my breath. Tomorrow I was to have the inestimable pleasure of telling my boss that I would not now after all be making banking my career.

Whoop, as they say, pee.

'Well, I personally think you're mad,' said Mr Grammer. 'What?'

It was Mr Grammer's habit to say 'What?' A personal mannerism that did not require an answer, or repetition of one's previous remark.

'Well, sir –'

'What?'

This second 'what' meant 'Carry on, I'm listening,' so I carried on. 'It's something I've always wanted to do, sir. As you know, I've been in an amateur company for about eighteen months now and it's just, well, what I want to do.'

'But it's not a very secure job, is it, Barker? Banking is a job for life. Safe, secure. A rise every year – by the time you're thirty you could be earning ten pounds a week, like Mr Day.' (Mr Day was the chief cashier, a man with the worry of the world on his shoulders.) 'What?'

'Yes, it is, sir, but –'

'What?'

'I have really set my heart on giving it a try, sir, and I've told them that I will start on Monday.'

'So you'd like me to ring head office and give in your week's notice and what not.'

'Yes, sir.'

'What?'

'Yes, sir, week's notice.'

'What?'

'– And what-not.' Suddenly I was enjoying the conversation.

'Oh, very well then, Barker, as long as you know what's what.'

'Oh yes, sir.'

'What?'

'What's what, sir.' Had I pushed him too far?

'What? Well, good luck then, what? I must say, I still think you're mad.'

I left the carpeted office, and trod once again the familiar creaky parquet flooring which led me back to my vast leather-bound ledger. Miss Jones, my bespectacled partner, and Hughes, her flaxen-haired fiancé, bore down on me.

'How was he?' asked Hughes.

'All right, really. He said I was mad.'

'So you are,' said Miss Jones. 'Wish it was me, though.'

I perched myself on a high stool under Mr Day's eagle eye, and contemplated the pile of cheques waiting to be copied by hand into the ledger. I didn't like this part of the job. To be honest, I didn't like any part of the job, but this part was dangerous. It was unheard-of to make a mistake in the ledger, so consequently the fear of copying down something incorrectly was paramount. Blots, smudges and inky thumb-prints were similarly to be avoided at all costs on pain of, if not exactly death, then vague punishments unspecified but presumably hideous.

To make matters worse I had recently invested two whole weeks' salary, namely two pounds seventeen and sixpence, on one of the first Biro ballpoint pens. (Yes, the pens we can now buy for 20p.) It turned out to be a great mistake, a most terrible purchase. It spluttered, leaked and deposited small blobs of ink both on the page and on the fingers. After three hair-raising entries in the ledger, it was placed firmly back in the top pocket of my suit, whence it leaked through to my shirt.

But today, I dipped my reinstated steel pen nib into the inkwell with a light heart. On Saturday afternoon I would be a free man. Just four more days of ledgers. Just four more days of Mr Day's benevolent but eagle eye. And only four more days of Mr Grammer, the Manager, and his jokes relating to the large wooden drawers containing cheques and statements presided over by Miss Jones, which had to be carried downstairs to the strongroom each night before we left.

I worked happily throughout the afternoon, closed the front door at three o'clock sharp, helped to balance the accounts and emptied the wastepaper-baskets.

The door to the Manager's office opened. Mr Grammer put his head round it and looked at me with a twinkle in his eye.

'Time to take Miss Jones' drawers down, Barker,' he said. 'What?'

Thursday night was Theatre Players' night. As I had reminded my boss, I had belonged to this amateur group for about eighteen months. I had been in three or four productions, and was currently rehearsing the part of Cis Farringdon in *The Magistrate*, a farce by Arthur Pinero. I arrived early on what was to be my last meeting with these lovely people – clattering up the wooden stairs of the unfurnished room above (I believe) an upholsterer's, to find only Mrs Bayliss, a tiny bundle of wit and energy, lighting the oil stove which was the only source of heat on that chilly November evening.

Mrs Bayliss had been my guide and mentor ever since I first set foot in the premises, having been introduced by my pal, Geoff Broadis. I had never even considered acting as a hobby, let alone a profession, before Geoff, a neighbour and school friend, suggested that I might like to join, 'For something to do,' he had said, 'just to paint scenery, or something. There are quite a few girls there.'

This last remark had possibly persuaded me, so I had turned up, been offered and had smoked my first cigarette, and met a girl called Kathleen. In a few months she became quite fond of me and I fell madly in love with her. We would go out together to the Playhouse Theatre in Oxford to see real actors at work; I would spend days at her house with her sweet and jolly parents, and we had lots of laughs. I would see Kathleen home after the Theatre Players' rehearsals, and there would be lengthy goodnight kisses; but in spite of the fact that we both regarded ourselves as unofficially engaged to be married, Kathleen would never allow me to touch most of her parts. And especially the parts I most wanted to touch, which were mostly the most of her she didn't want touched.

Now this, in a young lad, is bound to create the feeling that he is getting nowhere, with the result that by the time this final Thursday meeting arrived, the passion we first felt for each other had begun to wane. It would be with not too much regret that I would be saying my goodbyes to sweet Kathleen, or sweet FA as I had been known to call her during my darker moods. But not often. It had been a charming, happy and exciting relationship in spite of the out-of-bounds, keep-off-the-grass, mind-how-you-go and watch-your-step side of the affair.

So, here I was, greeting Mrs Bayliss warmly in the cold rehearsal room. 'How did you get on?' she asked. Of course she had known for some weeks that I was going to Aylesbury for the audition.

'I got it.'

'Oh Ronnie!' Her piercing eyes lit up. 'Oh, I'm so proud.'

She hugged me, her protégé, the lad whom she had coached in his audition for the Young Vic School, and who had let her down by failing to gain a place. This hug was a vindication of all that past disappointment. I had done what none of the group had done – I had got my foot on the lowest of the rungs at the bottom of the gigantic ladder that soars upwards into the distant realms of stardom. Perched up there, hidden by clouds, sat Laurence Olivier, Ralph Richardson, Alec Guinness and the rest. Were they beckoning to me? If they were, I wasn't aware of it. I didn't even look up. My horizons were confined to the Aylesbury Repertory Co, presented by Mr Armitage Owen, A Different Play Each Week. My mind's eye had only room to take in the glow of the footlights on the dusty red velvet carpet that in a fortnight's time would rise to reveal Ronald Barker Esquire, actor.

As I left Aylesbury, I had picked up a leaflet from the box-office telling of forthcoming attractions. That night in bed, I shuddered, half in fear, but mostly with delight, as I read, *Next week the outrageous farce*, He Walked in Her Sleep. *Monday, November 15th, J M Barrie's classic*, Quality Street. *Book early to avoid Disappointment*.

So my first appearance was to be in *Quality Street*. I made up my mind, then and there, that from now on, whatever happened, I would do my utmost to see that the public avoided Disappointment – especially those who booked early.

2

Curiously enough, I remember little about the first week of rehearsals for my impending debut in *Quality Street*. I was cast as Lieutenant Spicer and had two short scenes, one of which took place in the ballroom, here to be represented by a very tired painted front-cloth upon which was depicted draped hangings and painted chandeliers. I remember thinking at the time that everything on the cloth seemed to be very large and out of proportion, and thinking back, I realise that it had most probably found its way to us from a much earlier production of *Jack and the Beanstalk*, bearing as it did the unmistakable stamp of the Giant's Castle, even down to a golden harp in one corner and a gilded chicken in the other.

At this point I should probably make one thing clear. This was a tatty repertory company. Honest, hardworking, achieving excellent and entertaining results, but nevertheless well-worn, out-at-the-elbows, frayed-at-the-edges tatty. No one was paid any money to speak of. The leading man probably got paid ten pounds a week; I, as I have said, was on two pounds ten and Badger, I discovered later, was pulling in five.

I think, if I remember rightly, we were allowed three pounds a week to spend on props, which often included meals to be eaten on-stage. This enforced economy sometimes produced ingenious but revolting results. Lord Whizzby-Whatsits, sitting down to a breakfast of scrambled eggs and bacon, could find himself confronted with a plate brimful of custard and strips of pink blotting-paper. He would then, during the ensuing dialogue, eat a couple of mouthfuls of custard and contrive to bury the blotting-paper under the rest. But at this point I was not conversant with these tricks of the trade. I was a greenhorn, taking my first faltering steps into the world of props, scenery, lights and make-up.

On the first evening of my first day, the company gave its opening performance of *He Walked in Her Sleep*, an average pot-boiler of a farce, of which I can remember little apart from the feeling of excitement and tension pervading the dressing-room and backstage. A week isn't long to rehearse and prepare a play, and naturally everyone, from the Producer to the lowest of the low (which at this moment was me), was existing on prayers, Capstan Full Strength, and little bits of paper with lines of dialogue on, pinned strategically round the scenery. Alcohol, fortunately, is rarely fallen back on during these trying hours – not once during my time at Aylesbury did I see any actor the worse for drink. One old lady was certainly the better for it on one occasion, but she was a 'visiting artiste', brought in to fill a fairly small role and, as it transpired, to empty a fairly large bottle.

But on this Monday night, 8th November, 1948, everyone in the building (with the exception, possibly, of Jack Persich, the front-of-house Manager) was completely alcohol-free as the curtain rose to an enthusiastic audience.

My job was to assist the Assistant Stage Manager. I was, you may appreciate, rather vague as to what my duties consisted of. I just played it by ear, from moment to moment, taking orders from Badger or whoever, and trying to carry them out swiftly and efficiently. The curtain fell on the first scene. Not the first act, followed by the interval, but the first *scene* of the first act, followed as quickly as is humanly possible by the second scene of the first act. The curtain remained down only for as long as it took the stage-staff to change various things on stage to indicate a passage of time, and to allow different actors to get into position, and so on.

'Take the whisky bottle, put it on the table down centre, strike the matches, and put them on the piano upstage,' hissed Badger in my ear as the dust from the curtain settled to polite applause from the audience. Doreen, the Character Woman, hurried on, not at all affected by the dust, as she was already smoking her Capstan Full Strength. I rushed on with the whisky bottle, placed it on the table, and picked up the matches. There were only two in the box (doubtless another manifestation of Badger's economy drive). I struck each one in turn, blew them out, and replaced them in the box, which I then put on top of the upright piano upstage. Doreen watched this operation with a bemused expression and an occasional bronchial wheeze.

'Get off,' hissed Badger, and I got off fast, as the curtain rose. Indeed I got off so fast that I was only just seen leaving the stage.

'What on earth were you doing with those matches?' whispered Badger.

'I struck them and put them on the piano.'

'Christ, "striking" a thing means moving it or taking it offstage, you stupid sod,' he hissed. 'Eric's going to need those in a minute.'

Even as he spoke, Eric, playing the lead, sauntered up

to the piano, took a match out of the box and tried to strike it; failed; took the other one out; tried to strike it; failed, and finally glared off-stage through the upstage window. Windows on a stage never contain glass, of course, and Eric, seeing Badger waving a fresh box of matches at him, leaned forward and pretended to look out at the sky.

'Lovely weather,' he remarked, and put his hand through the non-existent glass, took the matches, lit his pipe, and sat down to play the piano. Eric had not rehearsed with the piano; being an accomplished pianist, he had not felt the need. He launched into the chorus of 'Some Day I'll Find You', and his face fell. The piano had been borrowed (everything was borrowed) from a local working-men's club and, apart from being desperately out of tune, it had one string missing, resulting in a thump rather than a note. Eric sat and played, 'Some day I'll (thump) you, Moonlight be (thump) you, true to the dream I've (thump) dreaming . . .'

This, coming on top of the hand through the pane of glass trick, was too much for several members of the audience, and a giggle began to spread around the house. Eric again glared at Badger through the window. But there was nothing to be done. Feeling as small as it is possible to feel, I apologised profusely to Badger, who grinned affably. 'You'll learn,' he said.

And indeed I realised I had learned three things in a very short time, namely: get off-stage quicker; the word strike doesn't mean strike, it means take off; and never put your hand through a pane of glass that isn't there. A year or two later, when I was wearing spectacles without glass, and eating half a grapefruit on-stage, the juice of the grapefruit spurted up into my eye through the non-existent glass. I promptly put my finger through the spectacles into my eye. A natural reaction, but it caused a few titters in the front row.

There were so many lessons to be learned. That evening I made no more mistakes, thank God. At the fall of the curtain, the cast, relieved at having got through the piece without forgetting too many lines and having managed their costume changes, all happily repaired to the pub next door to round off the evening, contented to be in each other's company and to let off a little well-deserved steam. I, for my part, was proud to be included in their number, even though I hadn't the money to buy a round of drinks.

It was only when I was alone that night in bed that I suddenly realised the full significance of what this repertory thing was all about. What had just happened to all these actors, happened every week. Every week of the year. They opened a new play on Monday, and on Tuesday morning at ten o'clock started to rehearse another, which they opened the next Monday. Then they started rehearsing another and so on, week after week, until the season closed.

And now I was to be part of this exhausting and enthralling treadmill. I lay there between the blankets and mentally took off my hat to each and every one of them. I would have taken off my socks but it was too damn cold.

The first night of *Quality Street* had arrived. My professional debut was imminent. The first act was over. The curtain was about to go up on the second. Behind the curtain, I could hear the buzz of the audience. They seemed so close. In a few minutes they would all be staring at me, the bank clerk from Oxford, the schoolboy from Cowley, dressed up like something from off the lid of a chocolate box, in tight white breeches that were wrinkled at the front and practically cutting me in half at the back. A moment of panic seized me. Would I have been better to have stayed at the bank, filling in the ledgers, emptying the baskets, and taking down Miss Jones' drawers every night?

'Stand by for curtain up,' hissed Badger (his life backstage was one long hiss) and I realised that, like it or not, there was no going back. The curtain went up, the dust rose, the smell of cheap perfumed disinfectant drifted across from the auditorium, and the lights hit me.

The rest of the evening remains a haze. I apparently got all my lines out in the right order, and could be heard at the back. I remember having my photograph taken by Eric, one of the leading men, in the second interval. 'Something to look back on, old lad,' said Eric, a cheery soul with sharp, twinkling eyes. The curtain-call too sticks in my memory; and the immense relief as I bowed, probably too low, at the left-hand end of the line.

'Well done, Ronnie. Are you coming to t'pub?' said Jane.

Jane was a student with the company. There were six girl students paying a pound a week each for the privilege of being allowed to play small parts and generally do all the dirty work around the theatre. They were all shapes and sizes, but Jane was the pretty one. Blonde, bubble-cut hair and tight tailored costumes, jumpers and skirts. She always wore tight clothes and high heels, to show off her legs. She shared digs with one of the others, Juliet, who seemed like a schoolgirl straight from Cheltenham Ladies' College.

'Yes, all right, I'd love to.'

I had been paid on the Friday, and had one and sixpence in my pocket after paying my landlady, and five shillings' savings, so felt solvent enough – provided Jane didn't drink large gins. She didn't.

'Half a shandy, love,' she trilled, much to my relief.

'Do you always ask men out for a drink?' I said.

'Only if I like them. I'm not fast, if that's what you mean.'

She was all of seventeen years old. I was allowed to walk her to her digs, about ten minutes away (nowhere was very far away in Aylesbury) and received a peck on the cheek for my trouble. That's good, I thought, I've made a friend. A girl, what's more. Even better.

In bed that night, huddled up against the cold (central heating still being for most ordinary people a thing of the future), I read through my part in the next play – J B Priestley's famous comedy, *When We Are Married*. I was to play Gerald, the organist, a young man in love with the daughter of the house. It called for me to wear my own clothes.

Clothes in repertory were a continual problem. It was unwritten law that each male member of the company should provide 'two walking suits, and a set of evening clothes'. Come to think of it, this was actually in the contract, so forget about unwritten law; it was written law. In practice, the law was sometimes bent a little, but with the exception of period costumes, very few garments were ever hired. In the main, people just borrowed from relatives. My personal wardrobe consisted of my pin-striped bank suit in which I had failed my audition for the Young Vic School, a green corduroy jacket, grey flannels, and my father's single-breasted dinner-jacket, the trousers of which fitted me neatly underneath the armpits. Eric, one of the two leading men in the company, also occasionally sported a pair of check plus-fours, left him by an uncle, which actually had a bullet hole in the back of the seat. When I asked Eric what his uncle had died of, he told me he was shot in the Dardanelles. To this day I don't know whether or not he was joking.

Alan James, the other leading man, was a tall, boisterous Lancashire lad who tended to play most of the comedy
roles – the Ralph Lynn parts and similar – varied occasionally by meatier characters such as Maxim de Winter in
Rebecca. Alan, whether light relief or heavy father, would
always wear one of two suits – his green, or his orange.
Admittedly, he called it brown, but it was most certainly
orange. And hairy. So, at the first rehearsal of each play,
Alan would call down to Horace, 'What d'you think,
Horace? Green or brown next week?'

'What are you wearing this week?'

'Brown.'

'Well, make it the green, then.'

'Right. I could wear my dinner-jacket in the second act,'
suggested Alan, 'to make a change.'

'But you're just off to play tennis.'

'Well, I could put a line in about saving me having to
change for dinner.'

'Don't be so daft, stay in the green.'

Ted Morton, the Character Man, had no dinner-jacket.
Instead, he had a full set of tails which he invariably wore,
sporting a pink artificial carnation in the buttonhole. On
one occasion, as I sat on the stage and Ted made his
entrance, I distinctly heard a regular fan in the front row
remark to her friend, 'Ooh look, it's still alive, Elsie.'
Which Ted, being partially deaf, failed to hear as his deaf
ear was towards the stalls as he came on. If he'd been
going *off*, he would have heard it right enough, though
whether he would have realised to what the old ladies
were referring is another matter.

So it was to be my blue pin-stripe for Gerald, the organist. I didn't enjoy Gerald very much. I began to realise
that on-stage I didn't know what to do with my hands.
This is a common affliction in new actors. It is the most

difficult thing of all to use your hands naturally at first. In fact some actors never conquer it. That stalwart Clive Morton invariably held his left hand down to his side, with his right arm bent at right angles and lying across his chest, as if he were escorting some non-existent lady in to dinner. Whether a colonel in the RAF, a High Court judge, or a noble at the court of King Arthur, he always appeared to be accompanied by this invisible wraith.

But to me as I rehearsed, my hands felt like two boiled hams hanging on the end of my arms. Into the pockets with them, I thought. I tried this.

'Hands out of pockets, Ronald,' roared Horace within seconds. 'Always looks slovenly.'

So I removed my boiled hams from the pockets of my trousers and folded them across my chest. I now had two bunches of bananas across my chest, but at least if I tucked one under each arm it didn't feel quite so bad.

'Stop hugging yourself all the time, Ronald.' Horace's beady eye didn't miss a trick.

'I never know what to do with my hands, Horace,' I blurted out, rather incautiously.

Alan James piped up, 'As you're meant to be an organist, couldn't you pretend to be practising on your organ?' This with a leer and a wink at Doreen the Character Woman, who guffawed, coughed, choked and lit a cigarette all at the same time. These sorts of jokes continued sporadically for the next day or so, but fortunately the script called for a lot of kissing and cuddling with the daughter of the house, and as she was being played by Jane, my new-found blonde friend, my hands behaved perfectly naturally, in those scenes at least.

She and I were getting on well together, and were already regular companions. The goodnight kisses were taking longer. I had to kiss Jane in the action of play, so we made sure we got plenty of practice whenever we could.

Goodnights, of course, could never be as long as I would sometimes have liked, because every night after the show was over, the pub closed and the goodnights perpetrated, there was still work for all the actors to do: namely to learn their lines for next week. Each night in bed I had to learn a whole act of the play, because each day of rehearsal involved an entire act.

For those readers (and that surely must be most) who have not acted in repertory, it goes like this:

Tuesday, read the play and plot the moves.

Wednesday, rehearse Act One.

Thursday, rehearse Act Two and run through Act One again.

Friday, rehearse Act Three and run through Acts One and Two again.

Saturday, run through the whole play.

Sunday off.

Monday (afternoon) dress-rehearse the play.

This was the pattern, week in, week out. The posters announcing next week's show went up each Thursday and on my way to the theatre a cold shiver would go down my spine as I passed a large hoarding advertising a play which most of us, as yet, knew almost nothing about. We had only rehearsed the first act! This learning of the lines at night incidentally meant that we could not cope with too much alcoholic befuddling of the brain after the show, so we saved getting drunk until Saturday night, when a good time was had by all (and so was one of the usherettes, but more of that anon). Sunday was the one day of rest and as I lived nearby in Oxford, at first I went home, exhausted, on the bus to my parents' house for a bath and then went back in the evening to my digs, ready to get up at

7.30 the next morning in order to be at the theatre at 8 a.m. to start putting up the set and decorating it etc, ready for the two o'clock dress rehearsal.

The digs or lodgings where I stayed had no bath, so the weekly one at home was bliss. The digs cost two pounds eight and sixpence per week, including meals, which meant that I had one and sixpence a week to spend. My mother, bless her, occasionally smuggled a postal order for a pound through to me by post, or slipped a ten-shilling note into my hand on Sunday, without the knowledge of my father, who said he would not contribute a penny towards my upkeep if I chose to be an actor. He was not against the job on principle, but thought it a rather irresponsible choice as a profession. 'Try and make a go of it, certainly – but don't ever come to me for money. You have to make it on your own.' I swore to myself that I would do so, but nevertheless couldn't resist my mother's secret hand-outs.

I was a smoker, of course, but could only smoke other people's until I got hold of the Abdulla concession. In exchange for an advertisement in the programme, the famous cigarette manufacturers sent every week a black and white box containing fifty of their cigarettes for use as props. Not all of them found their way onto the stage, however. Alan and Badger did not smoke, so I was put in charge of this wonderful hoard and used them sparingly on-stage, unless of course I ran out in which case I would substitute smaller, cheaper cigarettes. I remember Eric, the leading man, saying to me at a dress-rehearsal, 'Ronnie old love, I don't think Lord Eltham would return from a shooting party, go to the silver cigarette box behind the *chaise-longue*, and help himself to a Woodbine.' I got used to these rather perfumed cigarettes, with the result that when I was a little more solvent I started to smoke a rather exotic brand.

'What is that you're smoking?' Alan once asked.

'A Passing Cloud,' I replied.

'I know *that*, old boy,' he said, 'but a passing cloud of what?'

All this, of course, was much later, chronologically.

Let us return to *When We Are Married*. Although only my second play with the company, by this time I already felt that I was into the routine. I knew the company and felt relaxed with them. As you may imagine, they were all very different from each other. Doreen I've spoken of, she of the wheeze and the gasp, but a wonderful mother figure on-stage and 'one of the boys' in the greenroom. Ted, too, of the deaf ear and the pink carnation, who had a disability in both ankles, which meant that his walk was more of a prance, the foot dropping down as the leg was raised. At first I wondered how he could possibly keep in work with this – it has to be said – funny walk being part of every character he played, be it a lord or a dustman. But after a few weeks I ceased to notice it, and I can only presume that the regular audience did the same.

Roger, the other Character Man, was a true old ham actor, with I suppose forty years' experience in all sorts of touring companies, 'fit-ups' and the like, doing split weeks and one-night stands round the more obscure towns of Britain, and never, I'm sure, getting within twenty miles of the West End. Roger always knew bits of 'business' remembered from earlier productions, and forced them on us, saying, 'Oh, yes, it goes a bomb, this gag – never fails, old chap.' It often did, of course, and one had to slide it out of the shows unobtrusively, hoping Roger wasn't standing in the wings.

Alan James, green suit or orange suit, enjoyed himself immensely on-stage and off, and loved to make the others on-stage with him laugh. He was certainly not unique in that. There are always people who try to make you laugh; I have known them all my life, and of course have been guilty of it myself on more than one occasion. Let it be said that I disagree with it in theory – it often communicates itself to the audience who feel left out of the joke and so become resentful; you can lose them for several minutes. It can spoil a very good scene and is often annoying to the other actors involved. Having said all that, it is often impossible, due to the tension that is always present during a performance, to resist giggling helplessly at some inane under-the-breath remark, or an actor turned upstage and pulling the funniest face he can manage.

Alan was quite irresponsible in this respect. It never happened (mercifully) on the first night – he as well as everyone else was too busy trying desperately to remember what came next. But come Wednesday or Thursday, when everyone more or less knew what they were doing, he would begin his activities. Knowing the script by then, he could choose the appropriate moment.

In one solemn production – it wasn't Chekhov, but probably an older melodrama, the title of which escapes me – five or six of us including Alan were seated in an exterior setting, a garden or glade. An actress sighed; there was a pause, a long one, as required in the script. Her next line was to be, 'How quiet it is,' but before she could say it, Alan, sitting upstage at the back, made a noise. Not a very loud noise, but unmistakably a rude one. I will give him the benefit of the doubt and presume that he made it with his mouth.

There followed another long pause, longer than usual, because the actress dared not open her mouth for fear of laughing. The result was that, when she eventually was able to utter, 'How quiet it is,' the rest of the cast had even more trouble trying to stifle their giggles. Little moans and tiny snorts could be heard all round the stage. I had tears in my eyes, knowing I had the most difficult job of all, because my line was next. Summoning up my courage, I eventually blurted out my line, 'Not a breath of wind.' The whole company instantly broke up into paroxysms of coughing and hysterical moans.

The worst part of the whole affair was that there were three more performances to do and although, naturally, the noise was never repeated from then until Saturday night, each time we reached that point in the play the atmosphere was electric, and the pause tinged with hysteria. Alan, of course, disclaimed all blame. 'It wasn't my fault, old love, I was sitting on a squeaky shooting-stick.' But everyone still hated him for it.

He would also delight sometimes in saying a questionable word within a speech. The audience heard it, but believed they were hearing something else. He once had to say, 'I'm the only big bug round here, Jessie.' But Alan being Alan decided to make the word 'around' instead of 'round'. The result was that he appeared to be saying 'I'm the only big bugger round here, Jessie.'

Eric, the other leading man, was probably the worst giggler in the company. He was engaged to the leading lady, Diana Granville, who was, I thought, a cut above the rest of the company in the way of talent, though not at all stand-offish. I admired her from afar, much to Jane's annoyance. 'I don't know what you see in her, posh bitch,' she would say, so naturally I kept my thoughts to myself, not wishing to put Jane's back up. Indeed I had hopes of doing the reverse, namely putting it down on some convenient flat surface before very long.

The rest of the company, apart from Badger the Stage Manager, consisted of the aforementioned drama students: Jane; Juliet who shared digs with Jane; Cassandra, who lived with Badger and was glamorous and laid back (but only by Badger); Leonora, a dark girl of many moods, none of which seemed to include me; Sylvia, a kind, lanky comedienne and Ann Peasman, a street-wise, full make-up, no-nonsense-thank-you-very-much Northerner, old beyond her years. Six young ladies between the ages of sixteen and nineteen. 'Plenty for anybody,' I remember thinking to myself. Now read on . . .

3

As well as rehearsing and performing, I was now officially an Assistant Stage Manager to Badger, who I found out had only become Stage Manager the day I had arrived, taking over from Alan James who had until then managed to combine the duties of Stage Manager with those of leading man. Obviously the job had got on top of him and so Badger, being promoted, needed an assistant which was why I got the job.

I am still amazed when I think of it. After all, with no previous professional experience I had simply applied for and got a job. How lucky I had been. All through my career there have been moments of lucky timing which contributed greatly to my subsequent success in the business. This, then, was the first of them. The right place at the right time. So here I was an ASM without really knowing the first thing about it. But I learned quickly.

The job consisted of begging, borrowing or stealing the various props needed for the production. Choosing and persuading antique shops and others to lend furniture, and collecting and returning the same on an old hand-cart owned by the theatre; painting pictures and cardboard picnic plates to hang on the walls of the set; washing up all glasses, cutlery and crockery used on the set; providing coffee at rehearsal, and washing up afterwards; prompting the actors at rehearsals; making any special props not obtainable elsewhere (I once had to make a papier mâché turkey in twenty-four hours); sweeping the stage; striking and setting the props, and in some cases the scenery, during the evening performance. The list, as you see, could be described as endless.

However, it didn't take me long to realise that I had a small army of girl students who were expected to do my every bidding (insofar as it was confined to the production only, you understand) and I lost no time in delegating all the washing-up, coffee-making, sweeping-up, and other duties of a domestic nature, leaving me free to work my guts out prop-hunting and furniture-moving.

As you can imagine, a small town like Aylesbury didn't boast more than one or two antique shops, and previous to my arrival someone had obviously put their backs up, because they were never keen to lend anything except their tattiest stuff for a meagre reward in the shape of a couple of free tickets for Monday night. It took every ounce of such charm as I may then have had to coax ornaments and bric-à-brac out of them.

'Is it a violent play?' one shopkeeper asked when I needed to borrow a clock under a glass dome. 'Any fighting or throwing things?'

'Not to speak of,' I lied, knowing full well there was a punch-up at the end of the second act. On this occasion I made sure not to give two tickets for the Monday night, as I might find the clock repossessed on Tuesday morning.

The result was, of course, that there was never a vast choice of these items, and often the same ornaments would appear more frequently than I would have liked. 'Not that bloody old green vase again,' Horace would roar from the stalls. 'Haven't we got anything else?'

'No, Horace, sorry.'

'Oh, well try and stand in front of it when you're on, for God's sake. I dream about that bloody vase.'

A thankless job, prop-borrowing, and always will be. Not only that, but very strenuous physically. I staggered out of the junk-yard round the corner from the theatre on one occasion with the hand-cart piled high with garden furniture and statuary for an outdoor scene. I realised, as I began to try to push it up the hill across the square, that I had bitten off more than I could chew. I removed a heavy metal park seat from the top of the pile, put it down on the pavement, and trudged with the remainder to the stage-door. The electrician helped me unload the stuff and I took the cart back to pick up the seat. When I arrived I found it covered in old-age pensioners, eating sandwiches out of brown paper bags, sleeping, coughing, and generally behaving as old-age pensioners. They were very indignant at being moved off the bench, one old man saying he knew for a fact it had been there ever since he could remember, and he'd lived in the town all his life.

Rehearsals were almost perfunctory each day, in that everyone seemed only to be concerned with saying the right lines in the right order, and moving to the right place at the right time. Very little heed was paid to experimenting with mood or pace. The Director hardly uttered, except to correct a wrong move. 'No, behind the sofa, Doreen dear. Alan, shift over. Badger, move that chair out of the way. Does anyone ever sit on it? Well, get it off the stage then.'

The voice most often heard was that of the prompter, who was me, jogging the memories of the actors who were as often as not speaking the words for the first time. Some people could learn lines more quickly than others. The older gentlemen, Ted and Roger, were usually the last to get the words under their belt. Naturally, they took pains to hide the fact that they hadn't yet entirely grasped the substance of the role. Ted especially would pretend that something extraneous had momentarily distracted him and destroyed his concentration, whereas the simple fact was he didn't know the words. He would stop in mid-sentence and say, 'Listen! was that an ambulance?' or 'Horace, is this chair going to be here?' or 'Will these trousers be all right, by the way?' These last two expressions were taken up by the company, and Alan or Eric were always using them when they were lost for the next line. Sometimes they would transpose them so that you got, 'Will this chair be all right, Horace?' or 'Are these trousers going to be here?' It was my signal to come in quickly with the prompt.

My third part was Charles, the chauffeur, in *Miranda*, the story of a mermaid brought back to civilisation by a chap, and the unlikely and comic consequences of so doing. I was pleased to get the part chiefly because it meant that I would get a uniform, and so would not be required to provide my own clothes. A bonus indeed. In the event, the part turned out to mean a lot more than that to me because on the first night I experienced my first real big laugh.

The sound of the audience on that Monday night all those years ago is as clear to me as if it were yesterday. The thrill that I experienced on hearing that most wonderful of sounds! I get goose-pimples even now, just thinking of it. This is what I want to do, I thought. I want to make people laugh. Never mind Hamlet. Forget Richard the Second. Give me Charley's Aunt. My mission in life was now crystal-clear.

4

The time up until Christmas is rather a blur. I know that we did *Maria Marten*, or *Murder in the Red Barn*, in which the villain, William Corder, was played by the old ham, Roger. He came up with his best bit of 'business' yet (traditional, dear chap, and very effective), namely to be hanged on-stage. Simple, he said. The actor drops through the trap-door and the ASM (me), hidden under the platform, pulls the rope suddenly taut so that it jerks and vibrates most effectively. All the actor has round his neck is a false collar of rope matching the piece that hangs behind him. It worked too, and regularly got a gasp from not only the audience, but also from me as a twelve-stone man fell on top of me. At least, most nights he seemed to. It was not a job I relished. However, no permanent injury was sustained on my part or, indeed, any portion of my body for that matter.

The most satisfying thing during this period was that nothing lasted for long. One week, and then we were on to the next excitement. I really have no idea what followed *Maria*. I remember regretting not being allowed to play Daft Dickie, the yokel, in it – an early example of envy of the comic's role which I experienced quite regularly during the first few months. Eric played it beautifully, and the final words in the play, 'Hey, he can't be hanged – he owes I ninepence', brought the curtain down to warm applause.

Of course, the audiences *were* warm towards us – they were for the most part regulars, all having a particular night, and they enjoyed seeing which actor was doing what in each play they turned up for. These regular audiences were the backbone of the repertory theatre in those days. Television killed these little temples of Thespis without any doubt – which is a great shame. So much more exciting to sit in a darkened auditorium, watching your favourites being so *different* each week, laughing and applauding as a group; a sense of comradeship, familiarity, loyalty. I know all that sounds like a First World War recruiting advert, but every word is true. People loved to love you, loved to be a regular follower.

It was already near Christmas, and it was decreed that *Little Red Riding Hood* would be our pantomime, just for the week, of course; nothing was ever longer. A special girl was brought in to play the lead, probably because she'd played it before and had her own costume. This annoyed all the students, especially Jane, who looked right for it with her blonde, curly head and angelic smile.

'Why couldn't I play the sodding part?' said this angel through gritted teeth one evening as we walked home to her digs. 'I can sing and dance, I went to dance school 'fore I came here. I could do it on one leg.'

'Well, I should put in for the lead in next week's play, then,' I replied. Next week it was *Treasure Island*. 'Long John Silver sounds just right for you on one leg.' A handbag round the ear was all I got for my trouble. She soon settled down, however, except that during our goodnight kisses she suddenly remembered it again and kneed me in the groin. Aha! I thought, she's getting familiar; that's a good sign.

I was to play Trunch or Punch in the pantomime, I can't remember which – not now, nor then. They were comic policemen, and it seemed that we had to provide most of the script ourselves. Badger, the Stage Manager, played the other one, and we worked out various bits of business, walking very close together, me behind him, in step. Every time he stopped, I banged into him and we both fell over. It doesn't sound too sophisticated now when I think of it, and most probably wasn't. Hammy Roger played the wolf, Doreen the witch, Diana the fairy queen, and the rest is a blur.

Having exhausted myself playing Punch (or Trunch) with extra matinées thrown in, I also had to spend every waking hour making props for *Treasure Island*, as the Aylesbury shops couldn't provide much in the way of cut-lasses, hoards of treasure, or even a stuffed parrot. I asked Roger at one point if he would mind having a koala bear on his shoulder. He reminded me, quite rightly, that koala bears can't screech out 'Pieces of eight' at the right moment. God knows what we finished up with, but I suspect a couple of feather dusters got plucked in the process.

I was given three parts to play in *Treasure Island*: Billy Bones, who died at the end of the first act; another small role, I forget what, in the second; and in the third act, Ben Gunn, the castaway. What with struggling day and night with props and the like, I didn't manage to learn all the lines I was supposed to. I managed Billy Bones because he came first in order of learning; the second-act part must have been all right, but Ben Gunn in the third was, I must confess, a complete mystery to me. I can honestly say that never, before or since, have I ever gone on-stage knowing so little about any part. In fact, apart from his name, the one single fact that I could remember about the character on that first night (it got better later in the week) was that Ben loved cheese, and had been deprived of it for so long on his castaway island that he asked everyone he met for cheese.

The leading part of Jim Hawkins, the cabin boy, was played by Diana Granville, in a sort of gesture towards pantomime and principal boy, I suppose, although the panto had been last week. It was he, or she, with whom I had my scene, and she greeted me with some trepidation, knowing that at the dress-rehearsal I hadn't known a line, and that I really hadn't had much time between then and now to familiarise myself further.

'Ahoy, matey,' she began bravely.

'How be, young'un,' I invented. 'My name's Ben Gunn. I don't suppose you'd have a bit of cheese about you, now?'

'I fear not, good Master Gunn. Tell me, do you know the whereabouts of Long John Silver?'

'I don't know nothing about that. I was hoping for a bit of cheese, I was. My name's Gunn. Ben Gunn.'

'Yes, I know,' she ad-libbed, getting rather annoyed. 'I was told I might find him with that rascal Israel Hands.'

'Have you tried on deck?' I had seen the chance of a pathetic joke. 'All hands on deck!'

This made Diana livid, and I thought I wouldn't pursue this character further; I'd get off while I was still in one piece. 'I must go now and look for some cheese. If you find a bit, don't forget the name – Ben Gunn,' said I, scuttling off without daring to look her in the eye.

That night, two halves of bitter and a gin and tonic later, she finally forgave me. It was just as well she did for on the following night, while I was playing my first role in the first act (I knew the words of this one), the character Billy Bones dies of a heart attack when he finds the secret sign of death, the black spot, pressed into his hand by Blind Pew. He falls forward, dead, across the table. I then had to lie there for about five minutes until the end of the act. Not easy to lie completely still – five minutes seems like an hour. The trick is to relax completely as soon as you die.

I lay there for a couple of minutes, and then I smelt a strange, acrid smell. Something was burning. I realised quite soon that it was my wig. The candle on the table had shifted when I fell. The next three seconds seemed endless. What do I do? Get up, stifle my wig, and pretend to die again? That's certain to get a big laugh, probably a round of applause. Lie still, and let my own hair burn? Out of the question. Bang! A heavy hand crashed down onto my head. Diana, as young Jim, had come to the rescue. She patted out the fire, causing only a murmur in the audience, and I was able to carry on being dead in comfort.

I have mentioned Alan James' love of making people 'corpse' or snigger on-stage, and the last line of this scene gave him a splendid opportunity. The line was supposed to be a toast – 'A fair wind, a tight ship, and Treasure Island.' There was a slow curtain, as they drank. There is only one letter *p* in that sentence, and Alan made it sound like a *t*, but a glottal stop ensured that the audience didn't catch on. Not so the cast; they knew exactly what he had said, and even Badger taking the slow curtain down as fast as he could wasn't quick enough to disguise the cast's splutterings as they drank, or the sight of the corpse of Billy Bones shaking as it lay across the table. That's how the word came to be coined – a corpse laughing on-stage. Or so it is said.

*　　*　　*

In the next month or so, plays came and went, and I can remember little about any of them. I became Stage Manager, as Badger left the company and I never heard of him again. My salary went up to a princely five pounds a week, so that I felt really well-off at last. Jane and I had become very friendly, much to the annoyance of Juliet, the girl who shared her digs. I don't think Juliet approved of the way we carried on. Not that we were in any sense living together. I had never slept with Jane; it wasn't the sort of thing that one did on such short acquaintance in those respectable days over forty years ago. But we were very close and I knew that if I tried a bit harder, Jane would.

I was very eager, but the simple truth was that, apart from some ejaculatory fumblings with a farmer's daughter in an army dugout on the beach somewhere in Norfolk, I was in every sense a virgin. At nineteen! Well, now's the time to change all that, I said to myself. I don't know whether it was that Alan saw a determined look in my eye, or whether it was purely fortuitous, but one evening he sidled up to me in the wings and pressed a small square packet into my hand. It was pink and purple. He winked, and was gone, leaving me clutching the little paper envelope.

I knew what it was, of course. It was a French letter. At least, that's what everyone called them in those days. Mind you, they were never mentioned in polite society, as the modern condom is today. We called them French letters; the French called them English postcards – God knows why. Later, in the dressing-room, I examined it. This is the key, this shall be used to persuade Jane to consummate our union. I checked to see that Alan hadn't made a hole in it. It was the sort of joke he would have enjoyed. But I was maligning him. All was well.

In those days, there were ninety-eight pubs in Aylesbury. Jane and I would visit one or two of these most nights, and on this particular evening I chose one very near to her digs so that if she agreed to the proposal (or maybe proposition is a better word), I could rush her home before she had time to change her mind. Then, as we sat gazing into each other's eyes, the bombshell was dropped. She stopped gazing into my eyes and gazed instead into her beer.

'My landlady's away for a couple of days,' she said quietly. 'You can come indoors with me if you like. We can do what we like while she's not there.' Her eyes left her beer and looked quickly at me, judging my reaction. I meanwhile was surreptitiously feeling in my breast pocket for the little packet. Yes, it was there. Of course it was; it hadn't left my person for a single minute since Alan slipped it to me.

As soon as we were inside her house, she whispered, 'We can't go upstairs, Juliet is up there.'

Juliet always seemed to go straight home from the theatre.

'We can be on the rug in front of the gas fire,' said Jane, snuggling up. We were soon stretched out, entwined in each other's arms, with only the cheery light of the gas fire casting a rosy glow on our love-making.

'Have you done this before?' I asked as things began to hot up.

'Once,' said Jane in my ear. 'Have you got something? You know, a Frenchie.'

'Of course,' I said.

'Well, get it out quick, love,' she breathed.

By now we were mostly unclothed, and I turned away to do as she suggested. Now, I said that I knew what they were, and what they were for, but what I didn't know was how to put them on. I made the fatal mistake of unrolling it. This renders the whole thing impossible to put on and I was struggling in vain with it for what seemed like an eternity. Jane leaned over and saw my pathetic struggle.

'Come here, let me do it,' she said. 'It's come unrolled, you silly bugger.'

She plucked it from my person and I lay there watching her trying to re-roll the damned thing. At this point, Juliet opened the door and came in. She stared at me. I turned my back on her and tried to pull my shirt-tail down behind me.

'I'm sorry,' she said, 'I came to get a glass of milk, but I won't bother.' She turned to go. 'I think you're disgusting, both of you,' and she slammed the door and stomped upstairs.

Jane and I stared at each other, then got the giggles, and fell into each other's arms. The offending contraceptive was slung to one side, and I lost my virginity without it. Jane knew what to do. On looking back, I fancy she'd done it more than once before.

It was round about this time that I was roped in by Mr Wentworth to take part in a student production – a one-performance-only piece, rehearsed in the afternoon – as a sop to the six girl students. After all, they were supposed to be being taught how to act. They were paying one pound a week to the company, and in return did all the donkey work, acting only as skivvies backstage. So the student production, one Sunday night, was to give them and their parents the false impression that they were actually being taught something. Old Ted agreed to play a small part, and I was commanded to appear as the young man.

My main scene was with Juliet, who still wasn't really

talking to me since the incident with Jane at the digs. Juliet was young, about seventeen or so, and came from what I would call the stockbroker class; her elderly parents lived in Hampshire near the sea. She spoke with an upper-middle-class accent in a precise and articulate way – so different from her flatmate, my dear little Jane. She never swore or said anything of a rude or vulgar nature. She sounds a prig, but was in fact very sweet and shy.

During the course of the play we had to kiss. We discussed this, sitting in the stalls one afternoon.

'Have you ever kissed anyone on-stage?' I asked.

'No,' she replied. 'Do we *have* to do it?'

'I'll ask Horace,' I said. He said we did.

'We do,' I said. 'Do you want to practise?'

'Certainly not,' she said. 'I expect it will be all right, but not too hard, please.'

Kissing on-stage is not as easy as one would think. It is the most natural thing in the world in ordinary life, but on-stage everything seems to get in the way: nose, shoulders, arms, knees (we were sitting on a sofa), and even feet. We came to the moment, and cautiously manoeuvred into a suitable position, arms grappling nervously like a couple of gentle wrestlers.

'Well, kiss her for Christ's sake!' yelled Horace. I kissed her, not too hard she had said. I did it as softly as I could, and enjoyed it. As I began to pull away, Juliet pressed a little harder – only for an instant, but bells rang in my head. She had enjoyed it too. Her eyes dropped immediately, and she blushed red. After this first rehearsal, we discussed it again.

'You put your tongue out,' she said, but without any animosity.

'Sorry, I didn't know I did.'

'It was nice.'

The next moment is very, very difficult for me to describe. A blinding flash? Head spinning? These are old clichés. Whatever happened, the realisation took but a moment. I was in love with this virgin. She was adorable, shy, beautiful, and I loved her. Was it sex? Yes it was, but not only that. I wanted to talk to her, to tell her things about myself, to learn things about her, to be with her all the time, always. All this in a moment of time.

'Was it?' I heard myself saying, as if from a long way off. 'You're very sweet.' I kissed her again. I was slightly dizzy. She again looked away, but took my hand.

'Let's go and get a cup of tea at The Old Beams,' she said. We wandered out into the square. I wish I could say that it was sunlit, but it wasn't. In the foyer, the doorman, an ex-boxer with a face like Wallace Beery, growled, 'Mind how you go, it's pissing it down out there.'

The Old Beams Café across the square was a friendly, down-market, slightly cobwebby place where we sat, ate, talked and rehearsed our lines practically every day. Alan James stayed in one of the rooms above (bed and breakfast nine and sixpence). I once had to go over to rouse him when he was late for rehearsals, and found him fast asleep on top of the eiderdown wearing his orange suit. A cosy, homely place. But today it was different: suddenly very small, like a house that you come back to after years away.

Juliet and I sat at a gingham-covered table and I got the tea from the counter.

'Do you feel the same as I do?' I said, unable to take my eyes off her.

'I don't know what I feel,' she said, but she took my hand. 'I've never felt this sort of feeling. What about Jane? I was so jealous of her that night. You looked very funny, rolling about trying to hide yourself.' We laughed, and I

spilled tea on the cloth. 'Ronald, you're a dirty monkey.'
And that was that.

We were together. A pair, a unit. I felt awful about
Jane, but strangely enough she didn't seem too put out
when, a few days later, I confessed to her over a half of
shandy. She knew that there was no real love between us
– just fun, sex and companionship. I think if the truth
were known she had her eye on one of the stage-hands
who had appeared as an 'extra' in *Treasure Island*, and so
I didn't feel too badly about the whole thing.

'What about our date on Sunday afternoon?' I asked.

'Why not?' she said. 'Once more for luck, eh love? As
long as there's nobody about.'

My first starring part was the title role in *The Guinea Pig*
by W Chetham Strode. It was the story of a working-class
scholarship boy at a minor public school, and had just
been made into a very successful film starring Richard
Attenborough as Read, the fourteen-year-old cockney
lad. Being thin, baby-faced and of working stock, I was
ideal for it and seized my opportunity with both hands,
cutting my hair short and turning up at the first rehearsal
knowing every word. My mother, who always came over
on the bus to see each production, was rather disconcerted
when I had to warn her that her only son had to say a
very rude word in the play. The situation was that the boy
Read was complaining to the Headmaster (dear old Ted,
at his stoniest) that he had been ill-treated in the play-
ground by the other boys.

The Headmaster: 'But it is the custom that all new boys
are made to bow low to the statue of our founder. It's
tradition.'

Read: 'Please, sir, they only make you bend over so
they can kick you up the arse.'

The Lord Chamberlain had allowed this hitherto disallowed word after apparently much deliberation, because of the special effect the scene needed to have, showing how completely alien this boy's nature was to the cocooned atmosphere in which the Headmaster and his school dwelt. But not only did it shock my mother, but also the good citizens of Aylesbury. Of course, now one hears it in all American films *ad nauseam*, but in those days it was unheard-of in the theatre and, for the most part, in normal life. If someone was really a pain, they were never a pain there, it was always in the neck. So I got a few funny looks in the street that week.

Alan James played the marvellous part of the Assistant Master who stands up for and protects Read, and is instrumental in making him eventually into a first-class scholar. 'Good part this, Alan,' said Horace. 'Think you're up to it?'

'Of course, Horace, aren't I always? Green suit or brown for it?'

'You get a blazer and cricket flannels. Hired.'

'That's a treat.'

'And the part is played with a limp throughout.'

'A limp what, Horace?'

'You heard me.'

'Should be a piece of cake. My throughout has been limp since Christmas.'

So Alan limped through the play and was, as always, splendid. Juliet was now helping me enormously with collecting and making props full-time, and thoroughly enjoying it. We were not, in the physical sense, enjoying each other; certainly not to the full, anyway. She was a different sort of girl entirely from Jane who was, incidentally, already enjoying the stage-hand, as I had suspected she would. Juliet said she loved me; we were passionate to a point and then she would call a halt, as most well-bred girls of forty years ago would have done. I was content to wait, to bide my time, but she was so sweet sometimes that I could have eaten her.

Two important things happened about this time. One, *The Guinea Pig* was so successful that Armitage Owen, the big boss, decided to present it at Rhyl, in North Wales, where his other company was at present performing at the Pavilion Theatre, on the seashore near the pier. He told me that I would be going up there to play the part of Read again. The second thing of importance was the rumour that the Aylesbury company might be closing down. Good news, and bad news. In three or four weeks, this rumour became reality, so that by the time I arrived in Rhyl, I knew that I wouldn't be going back to Aylesbury ever again. I was sad, but at the same time thrilled that in a week or so I would be joined by Juliet, who had taken over officially as ASM.

5

I had arrived in Rhyl and was lodging in West Parade on the sea-front. The meals were not grand, and having had yet another rise in salary (to, I think, six pounds a week) I was feeling flush and thought I would treat myself to a slap-up meal. I bought myself eight ounces of best fillet steak and some beautiful asparagus, presenting them to my landlady, a genuine but simple soul, with the instructions that after seeing the present show at the Pavilion, I would be home to dine at ten o'clock.

The Pavilion was a great turreted barn of a place, and the actors were naturally all new faces to me so I tried to guess who would play what in *The Guinea Pig*. I hurried back to the digs, with the sea air in my nostrils, looking forward to my steak and asparagus.

'Oh, there you are, dear,' said the landlady. 'I bet you're hungry. I've made your meat into a lovely stew for you, and I've put your flowers in water.'

I sat alone, eating a fillet-steak stew, and staring at a bunch of asparagus in a glass vase. From then on, I ate what was put in front of me. Either that, or I went to the café along the front which advertised, *Egg and chips, one and sixpence, small children ninepence*. I never ordered the small children, but the egg and chips were excellent.

*   *   *

Rhyl seemed to me in those days to be no more than a very extensive front with nothing much behind. Rather like my new landlady. It was dominated by a large domed edifice in the middle of the front (unlike the landlady, who had one each side). The dome belonged to the Pavilion Theatre, where I was now installed. Next to it stood a skating-rink (roller-skating, of course) which blared out music for the skaters that was clearly audible in the dressing-rooms of the theatre though not, mercifully, in the auditorium itself. Except occasionally at a matinée, with about fourteen people in the audience. This must have been something to do with the acoustics of an empty theatre, and was technically beyond me. The music was faint and hardly noticeable during most of the show, but occasionally during a pregnant pause, the strains of 'Twelfth Street Rag' or 'The Cuckoo Waltz' would filter through, tending to amuse everyone on-stage except the actor who was actually pausing. Alan James, as one would expect, sought to capitalise on this by humming the tune very quietly, exactly in time with the record. As these were the only two records they ever played, we all got to know every bar of the ad-libs played by Pee Wee Hunt in 'Twelfth Street Rag'. To this day I can still correctly whistle every note. So you can imagine how mad these two tunes drove us, week after week.

However, I am jumping ahead. I was still in my first week of performance of *The Guinea Pig*. Having played the part before, having only three lines in the next week's show and, most important of all, being free of the onerous duties of Stage Manager, I found myself with plenty of time on my hands and until Juliet arrived, I was on my own. I began to explore the mysteries and delights of the promenade and sea-front.

My new digs in West Parade were two minutes' or so

walk from the theatre, and the commercial and amusement area started just the other side of the Pavilion. There
were various amusement arcades and a flea-pit cinema;
further on was a putting-green. The beach was long and
sandy, with its share of shingle and seaweed. It was still
very early in the season, but there seemed always to be
children on the beach, and the skating-rink played both
its records fairly constantly, even though there were rarely
more than two or three people skating. The water looked
grey and uninviting at that time of the year. As far as
I can recall, I never swam in the sea at all during my
stay.

The amusement arcades soon became something of an
obsession: the pin-tables were fun, but the wall-mounted
machines were more compelling. They would pay out six
pennies if you spun a ball so that it dropped into a certain
hole. And I was fascinated by the peepshow models in
their glass cases that moved – doors opening, ghostly
figures appearing, trap-doors, guillotines and all manner
of gory happenings at the insertion of a penny. They
seemed to me very ancient – and were then probably thirty
or forty years old at least, which would make them
Edwardian. I could wish I had one or two of them today.

I was also drawn to glass cases containing cranes which
could be manipulated from the outside to pick up and
drop objects down a chute into the outside world. The
floors of these cases were covered with liquorice comfits
and on top of these were the mouth-organs, lighters and
souvenir spoons that were the main prizes to strive for.

I was quite content to while away my free time during
that first week with these delights and after a particularly
good session one breezy morning, I began to head towards
the stage-door at about twelve noon to see if there were
any letters for me. The wind was whistling round the

shelters on the prom. Coming towards me was a couple: smallish chap, largish girl. A gust of wind took the girl's skirt straight over her head. She turned away and a button must have come undone somewhere because her cami-knickers went in exactly the same direction – up. I was presented with a perfect comic picture postcard of the ruder kind. The full hot cross bun, not a dimple left unrevealed. I quickly sat down on a bench so as not to embarrass the poor woman, and gazed out to sea. Behind me she was being straightened out and made decent by her husband, and I heard her say, 'George, supposing somebody had seen me?'

'No one would have recognised you,' he soothed. 'You had your clothes over your head.'

I sat still and waited until they had moved on, before nipping in the stage-door. 'Morning, Ivor.'

'Morning, Mr Barker. Is the wind getting up?'

'Yes, Ivor, all sorts of things,' said I. 'Any post?'

'No, but a lady phoned half an hour ago. I told her to ring here again at twelve.'

Juliet, I thought to myself, looking forward to hearing her voice again. It seemed ages since I had spoken to her. A few minutes later, the phone rang. It wasn't Juliet. It was Jane.

'Surprised to hear from me, are you? Listen, love, I'm going home. I've left. I've had enough. I'm on me way back to Manchester to see me Mum and Dad. I thought I'd pop up and see you on me way. Have to go to Crewe any road.'

'What about Roy?' (the stage-hand).

'I've finished with him. Dozy bugger. Don't you want to see me then?'

'Of course I do, Janey.'

'Right then, I'll be up on Friday. I hope you've got a

room on your own.' I told her I had. 'Lovely. Well, you won't be on your own Friday night. I've got to leave early Saturday morning.'

'Janey, you won't tell Juliet you're coming, will you?'

There was a snort at the other end of the line. 'What do you think I am, daft, or what? Tarra.' And she was gone.

There was not much I could do. Of course, it would be nice to see her again (for the last time as it turned out), but my love for Juliet made me worry that it would affect my physical feelings towards Jane. Would everything be all right? It was. I booked a single room for Jane, telling the landlady that my cousin was passing through Rhyl. Whether or not she believed me (nobody passes through Rhyl on their way to anywhere), she reserved a single room on the floor above mine which, it goes without saying, remained empty during Friday night and had its bed-clothes rumpled on Saturday morning.

The time came for Jane and me to say our goodbyes. She had an enormous suitcase which weighed a ton and had nearly given me a hernia getting it up the stairs the previous evening. It was full of everything she owned, all those little bits of her that I remembered – all the tailored suits, the short skirts, the high-heeled shoes, lipsticks, hair curlers. All the bits that, put together, made up my Janey. I felt sad, and marvelled how short our relationship had been – a matter of only a few weeks. She was the sort of girl you got to know a lot about quickly.

I sat on the suitcase and helped her to close it, then set off with it down the two flights of stairs to the front door. I managed one flight but on the second flight I tripped and fell. It was the full stuntman thing down the stairs, with the suitcase crashing down in front of me. I landed heavily at the bottom, with Jane clattering down on her high heels to pick me up and fuss around me. A terrible, sharp, agonising pain shot through my right knee as I hit the floor. A bang on the head went almost unnoticed as I tried to get up and walk. Red-hot pain through the knee again. I tried to make light of it, as Jane cooed and cuddled, muttering, 'Bloody suitcase, oh my love, I am sorry.' Her taxi was at the door. I managed to hobble to it and put her in, leaving the cab-driver to manhandle the case aboard. I kissed her through the window. She promised to write (which thankfully she never did) and was gone out of my life.

I could hardly put my right foot to the ground. Quick thinking amid the pain. Doctor? If I saw one, he wouldn't let me go on. We had two shows. No understudies; it was unheard-of in repertory at that time. No, I would have to hobble through the matinée and evening performance, and see a doctor tomorrow (Sunday). *The Guinea Pig* would then be finished and anyone could play my three lines next week. Settled. I crawled back to my room and put cold water compresses on my knee. It hadn't swollen very much, which surprised me. I would have to make up a line in the play about having taken a knock from a ball, to explain the limp. A limp throughout, I thought, remembering Alan's joke at Aylesbury. Good God, the *Master* limped as well, all through the play. Well, it's obvious; when I get to the theatre I must ask him, just for today, not to limp.

'You wouldn't mind, would you?'

'Of course I mind. It's part of my character.' He wasn't such a nice chap as Alan.

I tried to reason with him. 'It will look silly.'

'My dear fellow, it was you who fell down the stairs, not me. *I'm* not changing my performance to suit you.'

He was being a bit of a swine. My dear fellow, indeed.

The upshot was, of course, that we both limped our way through two shows that Saturday. It must have looked very comical, especially when I followed him across the entire width of the stage at one point. I know it looked comical, because it got a laugh. Mind you, I must confess I helped it a bit by getting precisely into step behind him as he went.

In the morning, the Stage Manager got me an appointment to see a doctor at his surgery in the town. A taxi delivered me to a rather imposing Victorian private house, where a charming gentleman introduced himself as Dr Griffiths. 'You've put your cartilage out,' he said, as I lay on his examination table. 'Painful.'

I told him I had done two shows on it, and he said I was a fool. As he examined the knee, he asked me how long I had been in Rhyl, and where I had been before that.

'Aylesbury,' I said, one leg raised.

'Oh,' he said, 'where the ducks come *from*,' and rammed my knee up towards my chest. An agonised yell from me, and a loud click from my knee.

'Get up, get up,' he shouted excitedly. 'Walk, walk about.'

I did. It was OK. That terrible click was the cartilage returning to its rightful place. He was delighted.

'It sometimes works, and saves a lot of treatment – sometimes even surgery.'

I was so relieved I could have hugged him. Instead I thanked him profusely, and gingerly went back to the waiting taxi. To this day, if ever I hear the expression, 'Where the ducks come from,' I feel it in the knee.

The following week I had three lines as a removals man in a play about which I can remember nothing. My appearance was five minutes after the curtain went up, and by about Wednesday I had achieved a record that was never broken during the rest of my career. I left my room at the digs, and twelve minutes later was back there, having performed my role in the play. No make-up was required – only a bowler hat, a warehouse coat – and I was on-stage. Two minutes' walk from the digs to the theatre got me there at 8.02. I was on at 8.05, off again at 8.08, out of the theatre by 8.10, and home again by 8.12. And for this trifling amount of time, I was receiving the princely sum of six pounds a week. That's ten shillings a minute! I thought to myself (quite wrongly, because I had to do eight performances).

The following week, the company, or rather a few of them, were joining us at Rhyl and the Aylesbury Repertory Company ceased to exist from that time onward. Alan James came up; Eric didn't; neither did Roger or dear old Ted. But of course Juliet, who was now an Assistant Stage Manager, came with them to take the place of a large girl who was leaving to get married. Everything was working out well. Juliet and I would soon be together again. I couldn't wait – and neither could the girl who was leaving to get married, judging by the size of her.

I went to see the landlady about booking another room. She was sitting in her kitchen, nursing a mug of tea.

'Come in. Sit down. What can I do you for?'

I told her that the girl I was engaged to was coming up to join the company, and had she got a single room.

'Have you consummated your engagement?' she asked.

I replied that I wasn't sure what she meant.

'Achieved physical union,' she said, and without waiting for an answer continued, 'I was consummated at sixteen.' It all sounded rather religious, and a picture came to my mind of consummation classes held by the vicar, followed by the actual ceremony performed by a visiting bishop.

'Consummated at sixteen, and then again at eighteen.'

I remarked that it seemed rather a long time between unions, and she laughed.

'Different bloke. I was engaged twice is what I meant. I was too young at sixteen. I broke that off. Then I met Evans. Consummated at eighteen, married at nineteen, widowed at forty-two. Now I'm fifty-one.' She looked every year of that. 'And do you know, when I got married, I was a sylph. A sylph,' she repeated, this mountainous woman. 'I'll show you my wedding photo. No, why I ask is that I've got a room next week, but only till Wednesday. So if you're consummated, you'd be better off in a double, isn't it? Saves money. Stands to reason, and I don't expect they pay you much over by there.' She pointed with her mug in the direction of the theatre and spilled tea on the floor.

It was true, it would save us both money. I decided to book the single room until Wednesday, giving me the chance to talk Juliet into sharing. Because, of course, the engagement wasn't yet 'consummated' in the full sense of the word. The weather wasn't yet dry enough or warm enough for a secluded field somewhere, and our digs had been out of the question when you considered my sharp-eared landlady, and the fact that until I left Aylesbury, Juliet had been sharing with Jane. Added to which, I don't think Juliet was quite certain that she wanted marriage to an actor; it's a fairly daft idea when you consider it, the state of employment being what it was (and still is). There was no question of a casual affair, on the other hand. Jane may have been quite happy to have a bit of fun without strings attached, but Juliet had been brought up differently.

In the event, she was so pleased that we were together

again that she eagerly accepted the idea that we should pool our resources, as she put it with a giggle.

'Pool our resources, enhance our circumstances and possibly air our differences,' I joked, and received a lady-like slap on the face. I countered with an ungentlemanly slap somewhere else. This caused a full-scale fight to erupt, finishing on the carpet of my bedroom floor. The landlady opened the door without knocking and said, 'Oh, I see you're settling in nicely, that's good. I *thought* I heard you,' and left, with a heavy wink to me from the door.

And so began two or three score of happy days in each other's company. Having, as the landlady put it 'achieved physical union', we were at ease, content and light of heart. Weekly plays came and went, but who knows what they were, or what parts I played in them. Juliet, I know, played the occasional small part – a maid, in crisp black and white with a silly cap down over her forehead. But my roles are now all a blur, apart from some character called Algy in some farce or other. It was the first time I ever wore a monocle, which of itself gives the face a sort of silly-ass look. I think I was creating the prototype of all the aristocratic old fools I've since played in monocles.

Even some of the lines remain with me. I said to the girl, 'What are you reading?'

'Tolstoy,' she replied.

'Sounds jolly good. Who wrote it?'

The hostess complaining that the sundial in the garden was no use as it was in the shade and my character answering, 'Why not bring it indoors and put it under the light in the hall? Then you could tell what time it is at night.'

The hostess saying to me, 'When are you thinking of getting married, Algy?' and me replying, 'Constantly, Lady P, constantly.'

I loved playing those simple upper-class idiots. I also played a police inspector and began to realise that they are thankless, difficult parts to learn and to perform – each speech is a question. Fine for the other characters – they answer the questions, and so get given their cue, but the poor old policeman has to remember maybe a hundred questions in exactly the right order! No wonder so many of them carry an open notebook.

In spite of the feeling of euphoria which pervaded my days with Juliet, there was an air of general unease, and rumours were rife that the company was on its last legs. The move to Rhyl, according to Alan who always seemed to know where the body was buried, had only been prolonging the agony. I think because he was a friend of both Horace Wentworth and Armitage Owen (the impresario), Alan got to know things a bit sooner that the rest of the company. It turned out to be true, too; within a few weeks, after a desperate fortnight at neighbouring Llandudno, the company finally folded. The famous Manchester Repertory Company was no more. Everyone said their tearful goodbyes and disappeared to all parts of the compass. I never saw or heard of any of them again. Except for Juliet.

She came to stay at my parents' home in Oxford a month or so later, and we had four or five days of bliss together. It was June or July, and the nights were warm. On the last evening, she suggested a walk through the fields near my house, fields which are now covered in factories, but then were ploughed and set with barley. She wore a long, brown and white flowered dress, in the style that was then called the New Look. In the corner of the field, as we walked, she suddenly ran ahead of me, unbuttoned her dress, and took it off as if it were a raincoat. She was without underclothes, completely naked, and she danced – ballet-school poses, steps and pirouettes – in the moonlight. Without doubt one of most beautiful sights I have ever seen.

I saw her only once more, a few months later. I had of course been writing to her, and she had been replying. One of my more erotic epistles was discovered and read by her father, who immediately forbade her ever to see or write to me again. When I did see her at her new repertory company in the West Country, she was with another young actor and I knew everything between us was over. She had been much too young and so I suppose was I. It was a wild and immature liaison, but never to be forgotten. I never saw her again.

And now, when I think back to that time in my life, to Juliet dancing in the cornfield under a warm moon and I see, as though through a child's kaleidoscope, the fragmented images of my youthful days, I realise how fleeting and precious is the nature of that youth. It was a silver time. I too was dancing in the moonlight.

6

Back home, and out of work. I have since heard actors say that the hardest job to get in your entire career is the second job. The first job sort of happens, and you are then a professional. But for the second one, you have to admit in your letter of application or your audition that you have only had the experience of one previous job. And so it was with me. Engagements were never easy to come by, even in those halcyon days with repertory companies in practically every town all over the country. You might think so, but not so. There was apparently always ninety per cent unemployment.

I would buy the weekly theatrical newspaper, the *Stage*, and search the wanted columns rigorously and carefully, so as not to miss a word. There were stage-management jobs, but always for experienced people. 'Those with less than two years' experience need not apply', the advertisement would say. For months I lived in hope, but nothing turned up. I applied for jobs, and didn't get them. I was turned down by Butlins. I was turned down for a one-night stand fit-up tour. But still I avidly scanned the *Stage* each week.

I also scanned it for misprints. This, even at that time, was a great hobby of mine. The printed word has always made me laugh and it is somehow funnier when the mistake occurs in larger type, in headlines or the like. That's why one of my favourites is from the *Stage* some years later.

The column through which I always searched was headed, 'Artists Wanted', but somehow in this issue the letters had got misplaced, and so the column was headed, 'Arstits Wanted', and the first entry was a strip joint. I include a photograph of the actual cutting which I still treasure, together with a few other favourites, just for laughs. They are all genuine, and collected by me over the years.

This game gave me something to do but it didn't get me any work, and money was non-existent. I lived at home and got fed, but after only three or four weeks of 'resting' I realised I must get some sort of temporary job. I applied for a job as a porter at the Wingfield Hospital, and got it. There followed about four months of regular, hard, but rewarding work with polio patients, which I will not dwell on here, as it isn't really within the scope of this book. I'm concerned here with my early life in the theatre or, at this point in time, out of it.

However, eventually the *Stage* came up with a request for 'an actor to join a newly formed mime company. Please apply in the first instance by telephone.' It gave a Hampstead number. I phoned and got an appointment for the following Thursday afternoon, at an address in Haverstock Hill. There I met Clifford Williams who interviewed me, said experience didn't matter as not many people were experienced mime artists, and we would be taught. Salary, six pounds per week. I accepted eagerly. Work at last!

On the train back from Paddington to Oxford I was elated, and also rather puzzled as to exactly what was required of me. The more I thought about it, the more I began to feel that mime was essentially only *part* of any theatrical performance. I had always felt this about ballet. Why don't they speak as well, I would always grumble to myself. Then we wouldn't need all those lengthy synopses in the programme. So very limiting. In opera, why must they always *only* sing? Tuneless recitative between the beautiful arias. Why not speak the lines? But, of course, all this was rather academic. Mime it was going to be. I will *so* miss the words, I thought to myself.

The two middle-aged women sitting opposite me in the carriage were chattering away in wonderful rural accents. It was a joy to hide behind my newspaper and listen to all those marvellous sounds! '. . . it's been such a bother, Mary, it reely 'as. Wot with the will, and the executors, and the probate or whatever it's called. All that on top of the funeral. What a palaver! Sometimes I almost wish he hadn't died.'

Perhaps I can persuade Clifford Williams to let us do a bit of talking as well, I thought. A new concept. Mime with words. We might manage to get it on to the radio. You need words, I kept repeating to myself. But by the time the train pulled into Oxford station, I was telling myself not to be stupid. I had a job in a mime company; I was going to tour as a mime artist. After I had learned how to do it. Three weeks had been set aside to master the art. Three weeks' rehearsal, starting on the 2nd of January. Was that long enough? It was all the time we had. I saw in the New Year, the new decade, at home, and on 1st January, 1950 set off to London to take up residence in digs recommended to me by Alison Malcolm, the Co-Director of the company.

Of course, I really had no idea what I had let myself in for. But on the first day of rehearsal I learned a lot more.

Firstly, there were to be only six of us – three men, three women. We were to set and strike the scenery, and take it with us by train, all round Wales. We were to do mostly only one night in each place, then move on. We were playing to schools, in the main. It was not going to be all beer and skittles.

The rehearsals, warm-ups and work-outs nearly killed me. The energy required compared with Aylesbury Rep rehearsals was like comparing digging ditches with floating downstream in a punt. Although at eleven stone, I was (it goes without saying) much lighter than I am now, I still found it practically impossible to do most of the feats of agility required of us. All the others, of course, were thin as lathes and seemed much more bendy in joint and backbone than me. The exception was Helen, a Canadian brunette who at least had some flesh where girls are supposed to have flesh. She too found some of the contortions fairly out of reach, at least at first. Peter, the German member of the cast, could get his head so far between his legs that I whispered to Helen that he was probably just over here to look up his relatives.

She and I tried to keep towards the back of the room but it is difficult to lose oneself among six people and Clifford, himself a former ballet-dancer and therefore amazingly supple, would make us work twice as hard to achieve the standard required.

'You can do it,' he would say.

'No, *you* can do it, I *hope* to do it before I die unless, of course, I die before that.' I would grumble incessantly in this way but eventually I found, after the first hour of agonising stiffness each morning, that I was actually managing to do the backward rolls and the splits (well, almost).

After, it seemed, about six months, the three weeks

was up. We had rehearsed, and we were off to Welsh Wales. In London, on my own, exhausted, I waited to board the midnight train. God knows why. Why didn't I travel during the day, like civilised people? My memory can supply no answer. Perhaps we had worked right up until the evening of our departure. Certainly I know that we were to appear the very next day at Dolgelly. Anyway, there I was on the station, with more than an hour to spare. I had a large canvas hold-all with me, and a theatrical wicker trunk, known as a skip, waiting to go into the guard's van. The skip had my name painted on the top. I still have it. It was full of all my worldly possessions. I sat on it and watched people descending from a train on the opposite platform. They were mostly in twos. I thought of Juliet, and wished I was in twos, instead of sitting forlornly in a one.

The couples passed by me, glad to be home. I watched one couple as they approached. There was something familiar about them. My heart leapt. Diana and Eric, from Aylesbury! They reacted in surprise and we all clasped each other excitedly. It had only been six or seven months, yet we greeted each other as if it had been decades. All talking at once, we immediately repaired to the station buffet and bar which in those days was exactly like the one in *Brief Encounter*, with the prim barmaid of uncertain years behind the counter. Several half-pints later, with my spirit lifted out of all recognition, the two dear things saw me off on the midnight milk-train. Their farewell cries ringing in my ears, I collapsed in the empty third-class carriage and almost immediately fell into a deep sleep, my head resting on my hold-all.

It is said that when you think back to when you were young, you only remember the good times. This I think must explain why my memory is so hazy about most of the Mime Theatre Company. I still have in my possession a *Stage* diary for 1950, with a few pencilled entries. According to these notes we gave our first performance at the school, Dolgelly.

Horribly cold ride in a cattle truck. This certainly strikes a chord of memory. We all travelled with the scenery in the back of this bouncing and bumping truck in the bitter Welsh winter weather. A terribly depressing start.

Stayed at El Shaddai (sic), *Horribly* (underlined) *religious.*

Town Hall, Holyhead – poor house.

The entry for Sunday, 22nd January: *Went to Bangor, wandered about all day, not much fun. Very cold. Went to hostel for the night.*

And it gets worse.

Portmadoc. Slept all night in waiting-room of the station.

We obviously had no money and were living a hand-to-mouth existence in the freezing winter's cold.

One item in the diary, however, I can remember all too clearly. It happened in Aberdovey. We were giving a performance in what must have been an old cinema because it had its own lighting system – an antiquated electric board at the side of the shallow stage. I had been designated electrician – the obvious choice, as I knew absolutely nothing about electricity, so wouldn't get bogged down with too many theories. We always used what lighting was available in these venues, and Clifford and I had pointed the few spotlights that were around in the general direction of the acting area. 'Better try them separately, before we run through the lighting cues,' said Clifford. I tried each one. Nothing happened. This, I soon realised, was because I had taken the precaution of switching off the mains before we started. I approached the mains switch, a huge old affair which needed both hands to activate it. Grabbing it with both hands, I threw the switch.

There are two sorts of electric current, alternating current and direct current. If you get an electric shock from alternating current, your body is thrown off the electric switch, or whatever. If you get a shock from *direct* current, however, you cannot let go. The electricity holds you to the point of contact. This was direct current.

As I threw the switch, I felt a searing pain through my arms and my whole body. I must have yelled or screamed, and Clifford dragged me off the mains switch. He said later that he had felt the current as he did so. I was lucky not to be killed. It couldn't have been more than a split second, because I came to almost immediately, with the others gathered around me.

'Are you all right?' they chorused as I sat up.

'I seem to be fine,' I said, but I was shaking all over. I was sat in a chair and given a cup of sweet tea, while the others carried on preparing for the evening show. In half an hour, I was feeling thoroughly recovered. In an hour, I was feeling positively energetic, and with a sort of excitement running through me. As we got made up for the show, I said to Peter, the German actor, 'I'm feeling so full of energy tonight.'

'Must be all that electricity going through you,' he said, 'like Frankenstein.' He pronounced it perfectly, as one would expect.

And indeed, as the night wore on, I was more and more convinced that he was right. The performance which my diary informs me was 'a rotten one' finished, and I was still as fresh as a daisy. It became a joke amongst the others. I suggested a night on the tiles to several of them, but got no takers. They were all exhausted. But not me.

I decided, as we were about to leave the pub, to find some night life on my own. Night life in Aberdovey in the 1950s was at a premium, but Dilys the barmaid told me that if I went down so-and-so street, I would find a working-men's club, and after much persuasion, which included a rum and 'pep', she agreed to accompany me to the place by way of introduction, 'but only for a few minutes, mind.'

We found the place and entered. The working men all looked a bit aggressive, but Dilys was a big girl and I felt safe with her. Her 'few minutes' turned into two hours or so, and at about one o'clock I left penniless and arm in arm with Dilys. I walked, or rather staggered her home, a few streets away. I kissed her on her doorstep. It was the only place she would let me kiss her. Next morning I awoke feeling like death. The electricity had left me. I was Frankenstein's monster no longer.

A period of dreariness now enveloped me as I recall, albeit indistinctly. The days turned into weeks and our salaries, due to poor attendances and lack of bookings, were cut from six pounds to three, from three pounds to thirty shillings and eventually we were on 'a shares basis'; in other words, money handed round and shared out as soon as we got any. The tour was a failure.

In my Cardiff digs, at 22 Clare Street, I became ill with a bad dose of flu, and lay in bed in a dismal room with no heating, and no food apart from a loaf of dry bread which got drier each day. A jug of water was all the landlady agreed to supply. I had no money even for aspirin. I lay there for three days in this condition, and still believe this to be the lowest point of my whole life in terms of misery and despair. The rest of the company were doing without me on a couple of dates in, I think, Swansea, so couldn't visit me or bring food or medicine. But I must have eventually recovered and dragged myself back to civilisation, because my diary (no entries for the Cardiff period) informs me that we went to Stockton, and then Durham and Middlesbrough.

What must all those miners and their wives have thought of this rarefied stuff? By April, I see that we had exhausted the north of England as a recipient of this form of culture, and the company found itself in Penzance, having no doubt struggled in and out of guard's vans with the scenery and props, changing trains on the way down. In Wales one Sunday, we had changed trains five times. It was a pity really that Clifford Williams had accepted this date, at the furthermost tip of England, because it was here that the Mime Theatre Company finally went broke.

What a shame, I thought, that we couldn't have gone broke in London; what a shame that we now find ourselves about as far away from home as we could possibly get, with not a penny between us. The moment the news broke, the same question was on everyone's lips. How were we to get back?

'Ah,' said Clifford, 'I wasn't stupid enough not to have thought of that. I have withheld enough money for exactly this contingency.'

A sigh of relief went round the company.

'I have enough for single tickets to London for five people.'

The sigh of relief was superseded by a cry of concern.

'There are *six* of us,' piped up Peter: like all Germans, the clear-headed economist.

'Yes, well, I couldn't quite scrape up enough for that,' Clifford replied lamely. 'One of us will have to walk home.'

'*I'm* not walking home,' announced Helen.

'Well, naturally,' I said, 'you live in Canada.'

This levity was judged to be uncalled-for in the present

situation and someone suggested that we should draw straws.

Straws were unavailable in the particular digs in which we were gathered, so Alison went into the back garden to find some sticks. We watched her mournfully through the windows as she ferreted about among the weeds in the drizzling rain. She returned with six twigs, which she concealed within a large bible that lay on the dresser. Helen, the Canadian, drew first. Her twig was comfortingly long, guaranteeing that her journey, at least to London, would not be on foot. Peter drew a second long twig. I was third. I selected one. It was short. It was the shortest twig I had ever seen. I've never *seen* such a short twig in all my life. If shorter twigs exist, I have yet to see one. What else can I say? I had drawn the short twig. It was I who had to walk home.

It was spring. I stood on the platform, watching the London train receding in the distance, steaming merrily on its way, and carrying with it the tattered remnants of the Mime Theatre Company. I never saw any of them again. I left the station, once more a free man. I had no luggage – Clifford had arranged that my stuff would travel to London with them, and subsequently be sent on to Oxford station, to be collected (and paid for by me, cash on delivery). The only thing left to do was get myself home. All I had in my pocket for the 275-mile journey was seven shillings.

So I set out towards Oxford, clutching a map and a small overnight case made of cardboard. The weather was kind; fine and dry. Exhausted by the end of the day, I crept into a field as dusk fell, and slept all night, waking, stiff and cold, as it became light. I set off once more, running along a deserted road to get warm. But the sun was soon up and I began to feel very hungry. I had a shilling to spare per day for food, I decided, as five shillings was reserved for a Cyclists' Touring Union bed and breakfast near Stonehenge. I had been advised not to go across Dartmoor on foot, so had to make a detour down to Plymouth, which seemed miles further.

Thumbing a lift was not yet popular in those times, except by servicemen. A smart uniform would nearly always guarantee a lift, but a long and tatty overcoat topped by an unshaven chin and overgrown hair was not an encouraging sight to the average motorist. But heaven be praised, a long-distance lorry driver pulled up in answer to my frantic thumb signals and gave me a lift all the way to Plymouth and out the other side as far as Exeter, where he bought us each a cup of tea and I spent my shilling on a pie which I bolted down with speed, relish and tomato sauce.

We continued to Honiton where I left him as he was going to Southampton Docks which really would have been well out of my way. I managed to reach my Cyclists' Touring Union hostel, where I luxuriated in a lukewarm bath of chipped enamel, accompanied by a lump of carbolic soap and the sound of an ancient geyser as it spluttered and spat above my head. The five 'shillings' charge included either an evening meal or breakfast. I chose the evening meal, having heard the clattering of knives and forks below me as I lay in the bath. I consumed the stew, or whatever it was (I was never told), with a great deal of bread and tea, and slept the sleep of the innocent, or in this case comparatively innocent, bearing in mind the two large chunks of bread under my pillow, lifted from the dining-room to serve as my breakfast in the morning.

The sun was up before I was in the morning. I left the dormitory, for such it was, and hit the road about 8.30. How I envied all those cyclists, leaping onto their machines and pedalling away down the country lanes. I slogged along on weary feet as they passed me, calling their gay goodbyes. At least some of them certainly sounded gay.

I managed to get a lift in a car nearly as far as Basingstoke from a lady of middle years who talked to me at length about religion. I incautiously let slip that I was an actor, which gave her the perfect opening to lecture me on the evils of that sort of life, suggesting that I turn to the Church as a profession. Her brother apparently was a missionary with the natives in Malaya. I thought of the marvellous howler I had found in a newspaper – the headline '*Curate served in Borneo*' – but didn't think it apt to mention it. I left her with the promise that I would go to church next Sunday, and struck out towards Newbury.

Naturally I stayed on the main road, hoping for another lift. I must have looked a really scruffy individual because I was stopped on the road through a village by the local policeman, who seemed anxious to know who I was and what I was doing cluttering up their village. When he found that I was genuinely passing through as quickly as possible on my way to Oxford, he seemed satisfied. 'Up at the university, I suppose,' he surmised. 'You'd better hurry up back and get on with your learning. Move along.' And he waved me up the road as if he were directing traffic. I moved along, taking a moment to glimpse my reflection in a shop window. He was right. I looked like a tramp. I was dirty, unkempt and furthermore, I was starving.

One shilling remained in my pocket. Twelve pence in old money. I came to a little country shop on the road a few miles from Newbury. 'Groceries and Provisions' it announced outside. Provisions were exactly what I needed. I went in, to find the lady behind the counter and another customer, a dumpy village woman, in the midst of a good gossip.

'He asked her to marry him. "Marry him!" my daughter said, "Why, he hasn't even got a wireless!" Yes, sir, what can I do for you?'

The dumpy woman said she'd be getting along then. 'Bye, Mrs Harris,' she said.

'Bye-bye, Mrs Harris,' replied the shopkeeper. 'She married my husband's brother,' she explained. 'That's why we're both called Harris. Now, what was it again?'

I had a shilling. I had to be careful. I saw beautiful crusty bread rolls in a basket on the counter. They were marked 'one penny each'. I saw a mouthwatering slab of Danish Blue cheese behind glass. It was marked 'ninepence a quarter'. Perfect. A quarter of cheese and three rolls equals twelve pence equals one shilling.

'A quarter of the Danish Blue, please,' I said, coping as best I could with the saliva. She carefully cut and weighed it, and wrapped it in greaseproof paper. 'Ninepence, please. Anything else?'

'Yes, I'll have three of those rolls.'

She gave me a smile. 'Sorry, they're spoken for. That's all I've got. Sorry.' She had no other bread. Nothing resembling bread. Cheese biscuits were tenpence. I paid my ninepence and left the shop in a daze.

Five minutes later I found myself sitting on the grass verge a discreet distance from the shop, eating my Danish Blue from the greaseproof paper, thinking of *Treasure Island* and Ben Gunn. 'I don't suppose you've a bit of cheese about you, now?' Cheese aplenty, good Master Gunn. But no bloody bread. A bird in the hedgerows chirped merrily. Twit! Twit! Ter-wit! he rasped.

It was three o'clock. By eight o'clock, due to a great stroke of luck which all things considered I was about due for, I was walking down The High in Oxford, coming up to Magdalen Bridge. A lorry had lifted me through Newbury and as far as my Alma Mater. By nine o'clock I'd covered the three miles home. I staggered in, exhausted, to the bosom of my family and had twenty-four hours to recover before my sister Vera's wedding on the Saturday.

I wore my bank pin-stripe. It was, naturally, a little loose on me.

7

Home again, in the Merry Month of May. What a luxury – warmth, decent food and time on my hands. Time to forget the rigours and deprivations of the tour. What a disaster! I tried to think what good it had done me, what I had learned. I eventually came up with two things. One, I had learned to do a backward roll – always useful when leaving a cocktail party unobtrusively, or dismounting from a bus in traffic. The other thing I still make use of today. Peter, the German actor, taught me to clean the marmalade off your knife before taking more butter. You slide the knife in between the two toasted sides of your bread, sort of lengthways. This leaves the marmalade *inside* the toast, and the knife comes out clean, ready for reuse in the butter. But, I had to ask myself, were these two tricks enough to justify the pain, exhaustion, and cold?

But it was all over now. A ghastly memory. I desperately wanted to get back to real acting, to the words. After a week's recovery, I was writing to the *Stage* again and this time I got a reply within a few days from Frank H Fortescue's Famous Players at Bramhall in Cheshire. Character Juvenile and Stage Manager. I had heard of these players. Frank Fortescue had many companies in the north of England, rivalled only by Harry Hanson's

Court Players. Hanson also had quite a crop of companies up there, and naturally they were rivals.

I had hoped to work for Harry Hanson because I longed to actually meet the man himself, on account of the stories one heard about his wigs. He had three, it was said, and he would change them according to his moods. If he wore his straw-coloured one, he was feeling benign, and his grey-black one meant a normal, run-of-the-mill attitude towards life that day. If, however, he appeared in his red one, then better beware: he was in a fighting mood. I presume that he knew everyone was aware that they were wigs and he used them as quite blatant symbols, 'like running a flag up a flagpole,' said Alan James, who told me about them. 'Of course, if he wore them at half-mast,' said Alan, 'it meant he was pissed.'

However, it was Frank H, not Harry, that I was to work for. Two weeks later I was setting off to Bramhall, with all my possessions in my skip once more. I was very excited. At last, being allowed actually to speak again on-stage. I couldn't wait to arrive and get started.

A nice man with the rather flamboyant name, John Pickering-Cail, was introducing me to the cast on the first rehearsal morning.

'This is Zelda, my wife, and leading lady.' A striking woman, about thirty years old, with piercing eyes and flaming red hair.

'Hilary Dean, Juvenile.' Pretty, Joan Fontaine-type.

'Vivienne Chambers, Juvenile Character.' Charming, gushing, eccentric.

'Olive Kilner, Character Lead.' Tough, Lancashire, white-haired.

'Olive is married to Alex, our Character Man.' Small, tubby; kind look to his eyes.

'Eric, Juvenile Lead.' Actor-laddie, affected, too friendly, obviously regarding me as competition.

'You're replacing Roy Dotrice, the chap who has just left, as Character Juvenile and Stage Manager.'

'Oops, sorry I'm late.' A tall man entered the room at speed.

'Ah, Glenn. This is Ronald Barker, the new Stage Manager. Glenn Melvyn, leading man.'

I shook hands with Glenn Melvyn, the man who was to become a writer, who was for two years to star in his own play in the West End with Arthur Askey; who was to make it into a film and to star in the film; who was to have his own television series; who was to employ me as a writer for that series; who was to teach me everything I ever learned about comedy. But who at that moment back in 1950 was merely the leading actor in weekly rep. I, who knew nothing of these future glories, saw as I shook his hand a friendly face with a twinkle of humour in the eyes. Tall and gangling, he collapsed into an old armchair on the set.

'Ruddy car wouldn't start,' he sighed. 'Had to get Joan out pushing it. No good. Finally I had to get out and push, and let *her* steer it. In the end I just left it, came up on the bus. That was crowded as well. No seats, I had to stand. I was exhausted.'

'You look exhausted,' said John.

'I know. Well, I must have done, 'cos a chap took pity on me. He made his missus stand up and give me a seat.' General laughter at this.

I found out, quite a bit later, that whenever possible, Glenn would always use a true situation as a setting for a joke or gag. I'm quite sure no one got up to give him a seat on the bus; he just couldn't resist the opportunity of a laugh. I didn't know it at the time but this was to be the first of about a thousand laughs Glenn and I shared during the next year or so. On-stage he was a riot, of which more anon.

John Pickering-Cail, the Producer, also played the leading roles, alternating with Glenn. Zelda, John's wife, was also, I discovered, Glenn's sister, so it was almost a family concern. Zelda and Glenn's father used to travel the music-halls as 'the man they couldn't hang', and I would imagine that as a young lad, Glenn had steeped himself in the atmosphere of the stand-up comics appearing on the bills with his father as they toured around the country. His love of the gag and the one-liner must have stemmed from all this.

He told me of a band rehearsal on the Monday morning where a manager had told a man doing an act with two pigeons that he was down to do seven minutes.

'But the act only lasts four minutes,' said the performer.

'No, no, I want seven minutes. I've got a bill to fill,' said the Manager.

'But it's a set act. It lasts as long as it lasts. Four minutes.'

'Look, I need seven minutes, and I'm telling you, you are going to do seven minutes.'

'Well, all right, if you say so. But I warn you, there's going to be a lot of walking about.'

Glenn told me the performer fell on hard times after that and when six months later he was booked for a show, he said he couldn't fulfil the engagement as he had been forced to eat the act. Another of Glenn's gag opportunities that he made sure he didn't miss.

Roy Dotrice, another future star name, had left Bramhall and in addition to taking over his job, I also took over his digs, just along the road from Glenn and Joan, his wife. The landlady, Mrs Holmes, a dear soul – large, motherly, and a sufferer from asthma – made me welcome and told me I had a lot to live up to.

'That Roy Dotrice was very popular,' she said. I promised to do my best, and in return she promised to feed me well and do my washing.

The Tudor Theatre, Bramhall, formerly a cinema, occupied a corner site on the main road of what was virtually a dormitory village for Manchester commuters. There was almost a countryside feel about the place, especially at the end of the village where the theatre stood. Above the entrance hall and box-office area was a small café tearoom, such as could often be found in these cinema buildings. A four-course lunch set you back two shillings and threepence, and was good home-cooked fare. The first time I ate there, I was served by the young blonde waitress with large teeth who regularly managed the whole place. I never saw the cook. I ordered the two-and-threepenny lunch, starting with the soup, which arrived with a bread roll and no butter. I asked for butter.

'There's no butter,' said the waitress. I waded through the meal, finishing with cheese and biscuits. They arrived with a pat of butter.

'I thought you said there was no butter,' said I to the girl.

'Oh, there's butter with cheese and biscuits, but not with the soup,' she said. In the weeks that followed, I managed to persuade her to bend the rules far enough to slip me a pat of butter with my soup.

I have in my possession only one programme from this era, and cannot think why, as now I am an avid collector of almost anything. But there it is. It is curious that I remember so very many incidents from my repertory days but fail utterly to recall most of the plays I performed in. I just have to accept it as a fact and nothing can be done about it. Not that it is desperately important; the productions I do remember are connected always with something that occurred to make them memorable. Otherwise, they have disappeared for ever down the whirlpool into oblivion.

So I began by appearing in some play or other, followed by a second, and so forth. I soon learned what the routine was regarding rehearsals, and more importantly my duties as Stage Manager, together with essential information like where to get the furniture and props from. This company, while still fairly tatty, was a cut above Aylesbury and each week the scenery came from Frank H Fortescue's central store in Manchester, where his headquarters were. It was my job on Wednesday afternoon, after I had had time to work out what was needed, to go by bus to Chorlton-cum-Hardy, to a large second-hand furniture and bric-à-brac shop where we had a hire arrangement. Crossdale's it was called, run by a large, bluff chap with a wonderful accent. He employed a rather dopey assistant, but I generally got everything I picked out, although I once ordered 'a dozen leather-bound books' and was presented on Monday morning with six pairs of army boots.

'Oh, books! Ecky thoomp, I can't read me own writing,' said the dopey one.

There was always the shop round the corner from the theatre to fall back on, which also belonged to Mr Crossdale and through which, presumably, the theatre got to know of his main premises in Chorlton. This was a much smaller shop with no furniture to speak of, just bric-à-brac. It was presided over by a Mrs Barraclough, a woman who looked just like Flora Robson. We struck up an immediate friendship. I told her of the dopey chap's mistake with the boots, and she said, 'Oh, him. He's an absolute barmpot, him. If his brains were made of gunpowder, there'd not be enough of them to blow his hat off.' This endeared her to me even more, and I always enjoyed a cigarette and a chat with her, time permitting.

Frank Wright, the electrician, a heavy, curly-haired man with a very dark beard-line and no teeth, came from that part of the world where the inhabitants mix up the letters *t* and *k*. For some reason he made tea up in the circle of the theatre and would say to me, 'I'm just going up to the cirtle to put kekkle on.' He was a great worker, and loved the theatre and the shows. 'Gorra gerrit right, Ron,' he'd say on the first night, or at the hurried dress-rehearsal on Monday afternoon.

For my part, that's what I was determined to do, especially with regard to the stage-management, because so many other people relied on me. Playing a part in the show, whether big or small, became almost a sideline, although of course I played important parts and relished them. But they seemed to take care of themselves providing I learned the words; I simply gave as good a performance as I could and didn't worry about it. Stage-management on the other hand was of necessity always a worry. So many things could go wrong and, in the end, it was always me that had to accept responsibility for it.

Doorknobs, for instance. They were always firm favourites; you could rely on them to misbehave. Doors on scenery never fit once you've got them up. They refuse to close properly and often, at dress rehearsal, you would make a dramatic exit, only to bump into a stage carpenter working in the doorway. For this reason, doorknobs were often the last things to get fixed in position on a set and were sometimes forgotten altogether in the first-night rush. Doorknobs would come off in people's hands as they entered. The unfortunate actor would burst into the room clutching one. Worse still, they would come off as you tried to leave the stage.

Zelda, the leading lady, playing Elizabeth Bennett in *Pride and Prejudice*, uttered the line, 'I must visit Mr Darcy at once. No time is to be lost,' and grabbed the doorknob which came off. The door, of course, is then impossible to open from the on-stage side.

'But wait,' she ad-libbed as she crossed to the other side, to where I sat in the wings at the prompter's desk. 'Should I go, or shouldn't I?'

I grabbed the ASM. 'Go and open the door, quick!'

'Am I afraid to go?' soldiered on Zelda. 'Is this the cause of my indecision?'

She brandished the doorknob at me and the suspicion of a titter that was building in the audience increased slightly, only to build into a full-sized giggle as the offending door opposite suddenly opened wide of its own volition.

'I *will* go,' said Zelda, and swept decisively off the stage followed by a round of applause from the audience.

'How heartless to applaud that,' I said to myself. But audiences are. If a dramatic moment is shattered by some accident such as this, then they will laugh. No sympathy is shown. They take no prisoners. Audiences are in turn loved and hated by actors. On this occasion, naturally, Zelda hated them, and wasn't too pleased with me either.

'Bloody doorknobs, why are they never fixed?' she hissed at me as she went past on the way to her dressing-room, her eyes ablaze.

'Sorry, Zelda. Frank must have forgotten to screw it on properly.'

'I'll screw *him* properly,' she said, and marched towards the exit to the dressing-rooms. She reached the door, then marched back to me. 'Metaphorically, only, of course,' she said, and poked me in the ribs. She was a girl to be reckoned with. Older than me, and not my type. But I would still rather have slept with her with nothing on than Frank in his best suit.

8

My dressing-room was to be shared with Alex, Eric and Glenn. As there wasn't room enough for the three of them, let alone a fourth, I decided to make my own dressing area in the big prop-room under the stage. It was almost soundproof, so I could change and make up there without being heard, but was still able to hear a muffled version of the play going on above my head. It was a real glory-hole, full of all sorts of rubbish, most of which looked as if it had been there since before the Flood – in fact I actually found a pair of mice sitting in a corner, obviously having missed the boat. But I cleared myself a space and propped up a mirror under one of the bare bulbs which hung down over the tables. This was fine; I could spread out here. Having enough space is such a luxury.

The work was hard, and I had to cope practically single-handed. No girl students here. How I longed for Juliet's help. Originally the ASM had been Sonia, the grand-daughter of the big boss himself, but after she left there had been two or three replacements who only seemed to last a couple of weeks before getting their marching orders. I think John, the Producer, was looking for a good actress as well as a backstage help, and they didn't seem to come up to scratch. With the exception of one scruffy-looking girl who scratched herself all the time, and who could easily have been acted off the stage by any chimpanzee with a fortnight's coaching in drama.

But, and it was a big But, she was efficient. She worked happily alongside me. All I had to do was make sure I kept her slightly downwind. She was not an ugly girl, but the poor thing would always lack male company. I think it is one of life's tragedies that practically no one has the courage to come right out and tell another person that they have BO. There, you see, even in print it is a shock. But what a service they would be doing to the sufferer, not to mention the rest of the neighbourhood. In the same breath, I have to mention garlic. Garlic is wonderful to eat but should be made illegal on the grounds of its antisocial consequences.

But let me discard this rather unsavoury hobby-horse of mine. Suffice it to say that I have never been brave enough to tell anyone that they smell, so should certainly not be casting the first stone.

The main thing was that the girl did her job very well. Clean cups, prop lists made out, props set on the stage at the right time and the right place. Life was settling down nicely.

Except, of course, that I had no girlfriend. Nor did I attempt to do anything about it, because it seemed that life was far too busy for me to be bored. I certainly made friends quickly and easily with most of the company, apart from John and Zelda who were very sweet but tended to keep themselves to themselves a little, and necessarily so, I think, being Producer and Producer's wife. It doesn't do in my opinion for a Director to get too chummy with the cast, as some will take advantage.

I became especially friendly with Glenn Melvyn, mainly

because he laughed a lot and made me laugh a lot. He was the most popular member of the company as far as the audiences were concerned, and invariably got a murmur of approval when he made his first entrance in a play. But a very modest, almost shy man to meet at first. He soon realised that I was always ready for a laugh and after a few weeks we became pals. It was he who introduced me to snooker.

The Victoria Arms pub on the corner at the other end of the main street was the only pub in Bramhall, which meant that all the funny old characters you find in all the pubs in a village were packed into one eccentric bundle. There was very little passing trade, so all the customers were regulars. Most of them, the older ones at least, congregated in the back room, where stood a full-size billiard table, surrounded on all sides by settles against the wall where all these old codgers were perched, watching and commenting on the games in progress. They rarely smiled, but continually made terribly funny remarks. No raucous laughter, hardly a face would crack, but the comic commentary would continue almost non-stop. Consequently, it was a pretty daunting prospect to stand in front of this panel of inquisitors trying to learn the game, never having handled a billiard-cue in my life. But Glenn, who was known and respected as a very fine player, warned them off.

'He's only learning, so leave him alone,' he told them, and in the event they became very helpful, offering advice without derision providing, of course, you bought them a round of drinks now and again.

I grew to love the game, and we played most lunchtimes. At night there was a different crowd in there, so we confined ourselves to the main bar, which also had its selection of regular eccentric wits. A pint of bitter, sometimes (but rarely) two and, even more rarely, a barley wine to go in it. This was sold in third-of-a-pint bottles, called nips, and is a very strong beer.

'Singing beer, that is,' said an old Geordie with a squashed trilby perched on top of a squashed face. He would then start to sing – always the same song which appeared to be a version of 'Here We Are Again' but was, in fact, an unrecognisable travesty which bore no resemblance to the original song.

'So here we are, then, so here we are, every day we're on our way, you've got to be happy and you've got to sing – so here we are then, so here we are!'

This was the complete lyric and we all had to learn this version and lump it. Having had our barley wine, we were quite happy to do this, and would all chorus with Geordie, which pleased him enormously.

Glenn was the only one in the company to own a car and he would drive me back to within a few yards of my digs and, on the nights when we hadn't had any singing beer, we would soberly enjoy a singsong, maybe for up to an hour at a stretch. Having been a choirboy, I was full of church harmonies, so we would practise on a favourite thirties or forties classic. 'My Heart Stood Still' or 'Just the Way You Look Tonight' or perhaps 'They Can't Take That Away From Me'. Memorable moments.

Glenn was the best and funniest ad-libber I have ever known, with the possible exception of the late Ted Ray. In later productions, if he and I were in a comedy, our scenes together got longer and longer throughout the week as we added little bits to each performance. The jokes that Glenn added were probably remembered in part from his music-hall days with his parents, heard from the wings while he watched the top of the bill, the stand-up comic.

He once said to me, in the middle of a scene in which

we were playing two drunken Scotsmen, 'Do you know, I've got two hundred more bones in my body than you have.'

'How's that then?' said I.

'I had a kipper for my breakfast,' he said.

This joke remains one of my favourites, and I used it in a *Two Ronnies* script some thirty years later; it still got an enormous laugh. A joke that's funny will always be funny.

However, I have to say a word at this point about adding bits and pieces to a play. In some of them, as in the one with the two Scotsmen, it can only improve it. But with a good play, it can obscure the story and make a hotch-potch of a particular scene. It all depends on the quality of the writing in the first place. But it has always been done; even Shakespeare had cause to complain about bits added to his script, especially by the comics. Mind you, his low comedians had stuff to say which nowadays is so dated that it is completely unfunny in the main, and nearly all laughs stem from the bits of business put in between the words. But in his own time, he even went so far as to put his complaints into words in *Hamlet*.

Hamlet is talking to the leader of a group of actors who have turned up to perform a play. He says:

. . . and let those that play your clowns speak no more than is set down for them. For there be of them that will themselves laugh, to set on some quantity of barren spectators to laugh too, though in the meantime some necessary question of the play be then to be considered; that's villainous! and shows a most pitiful ambition in the fool that uses it.

The master has spoken. Many lesser writers, I know, will agree with this cry from the heart.

*　　　*　　　*

A new girl had arrived. Annie Merrill came to do two or three plays which needed an extra woman. She was a big girl of twenty-five or so, not fat but tall and heavy; what the Edwardians would call a handsome woman. From the first moment we met, we both knew we would get on well together. She had a broad smile and loud laugh which opened her mouth wide. By the second or third day of rehearsal, we were bosom pals and she certainly had the bosom for it. About forty-two inches and difficult to describe without using your hands. She was enormous fun and as we talked in the pub in the evenings, I realised what an intelligent and well-adjusted person she was. She was mad on the cinema, as I was. We sat for ages outside the pub one night after closing time, discussing Olivier's film of *Hamlet* which was, she said, her favourite film. I think we had both seen it three times by then and we discussed favourite speeches from it. I told her about the speech I've just quoted in these pages, but that perhaps my favourite begins: *O, what a rogue and peasant slave am I* and finishes:

The play's the thing,
Wherein I'll catch the conscience of the king.

She replied, indicating her ample hips, that hers was: *O, that this too too solid flesh would melt . . .*

She really was 'one of the boys', as they say; a great sport. Not really my type physically; in fact I think I was scared I might get lost in that capacious bosom, suffocated in the grip of those muscular arms. But her dimpled cheeks were so pretty in a larger-than-life way that there was certainly an attraction there, and I sought her company at every opportunity.

The first play in which Annie and I acted together was a farce about spies in a seaside holiday resort hotel. The stage furniture had to include a chesterfield settee (which

The photograph that got me my first job in show business.
Looking at it now, with the black shirt and the yellow tie with
horses' heads on, I'm amazed I even got started.

COUNTY THEATRE

Telephone 13 **AYLESBURY**

(FORMERLY THE NEW MARKET THEATRE)

LESSEE and LICENSEE	-	-	-	**W. ARMITAGE OWEN.**
GENERAL MANAGER	-	-	-	**JACK PERSICH.**
PRODUCER	-	-	-	**HORACE WENTWORTH.**

The amateur dramatic bank clerk, a few months before
joining the Aylesbury Repertory Company.

Lieutenant Spicer in *Quality Street*. Photographed a few minutes
before my debut as a professional actor.

I loved playing comic clergymen. This one, the Revd Robert
Spalding in *The Private Secretary*, carried in his arms throughout
the play seven props, and was never allowed to put them down. A
wonderful part.

(above) My first role at the Playhouse, Oxford. With Christine Pollon in *Pick-up Girl*. (below) Christine and me again, in Anouilh's *Point of Departure*.

(above) Donald Houston plays his violin in *Golden Boy*. I'm the Jewish-Italian taxi-driver on the bed. (below) In the Gordon Harker part in *Saloon Bar*, I compare knees with Tony Church. Billie Whitelaw looks on, conveying a mixture of admiration and disgust.

As the gipsy man with three little troupers in *Listen to the Wind*. Photographed on this occasion by the great Angus McBean.

I leave the Playhouse – older and perhaps a little wiser.

has arms the same height as the back). This particular shape was needed for special 'business' in the play: many people sitting on the arms, falling backwards over the back of it, and other hilarious but dangerous stunts. This type of settee is difficult to obtain at the best of times, and the only one available at Crossdale's was one which had a loose cover of violent purple, flowered material. I told Mr Crossdale that the cover might have to go, but he said, 'God no, Ronnie, you can't take it off, the settee's in a shocking state underneath. I just hope it survives the week, that's all.' I tested the back and arms by sitting on them and they seemed strong enough.

'Well, it will have to stay purple then,' I said.

Luckily the set was in various shades of pale blue and cream, so at the dress-rehearsal the settee didn't look too bad. That was before Annie came onto the set. She was wearing an amazingly eye-popping creation. A sort of all-in-one jump suit cut so low in the front that it revealed cleavage down to the waist, and so tight at the back that when she turned and walked away, her behind looked like two little pigs fighting under a blanket. It was terrific, but it was also bright orange. Annie and the settee screamed at each other.

'Good heavens, you can't wear that!' gasped John in dismay. 'Not with that sofa.'

'It's the only thing I've got,' said Annie, adding firmly, 'I'm wearing it.'

John called to me, 'Ronnie, that purple cover will have to go.'

'It can't, John – the upholstery underneath is in a terrible state. Nowhere near as good as Annie's,' I added, which brought a wink of approval from the vision in orange. John pulled a face.

'Well, all I can say is, thank God it's a farce. What can't be cured must be endured. Come on, let's start.'

So the settee cover remained on. The settee itself survived people bouncing about on it and falling over the back of it very well during the week. I was the one, incidentally, who was doing most of the cavorting on it, as I was playing opposite Annie as the friend she was pretending to be on honeymoon with, in order to deceive the man we both suspected as being a private detective, who actually turned out to be a spy. (This, you may be glad to hear, is quite a straightforward plot for a farce.)

During Act Two, I would be sitting on the arm of the settee; she sat on the seat. The spy was heard to call off-stage, and Annie's line was, 'Quick, he's coming! Pretend to make love to me.'

I would bounce down off the arm onto the seat, and my face would fall into her overample and almost bare bosom. I contrived to make a sort of strangled gulp which sounded like my face hitting her boobs. A kind of 'splat' which got a big laugh.

On the final performance, everything is always a little bit overdone; it's Saturday night and the cast always enjoy themselves in a comedy. Annie was looking particularly seductive and as I bounced off the arm of the settee and landed on the seat, my face buried in her chest, something snapped. It was the webbing inside the sofa. There was a twang and a violent pain shot through the seat of my pants. A spring had burst through the material and hit me in a most tender spot, or rather two of my most tender spots. The agony was indescribable.

Fortunately my moans were muffled by Joan's pneumatic bosom. During the laughter, when I was able to get my breath, I whispered faintly to Annie what had happened. She didn't giggle and as the other actor entered we had to pretend to kiss and cuddle, which she did, as always, in a most uninhibited fashion. After looking round, the actor would leave, and we would continue the complicated plot. We would spring apart and she would say, 'He's gone. Go as quickly as you can and I'll come to your room as soon as the fuss has died down.'

I rose to leave and I found I couldn't. The spring had penetrated my trousers. 'Sit down,' I ad-libbed, 'I think he's coming back.'

She knew something was amiss; she could see it in my eyes.

'Let's cuddle some more, I'm getting to like it,' I said and we recommenced our grappling, much to the delight of the audience.

During their laughter I was able to whisper in her ear that the spring had attached itself. This time she *did* giggle. She was a real trouper, however. She slid her hand underneath me as we embraced, and after a great deal of wriggling and tweaking, mainly of the spring, she managed to free my trousers from its spiteful grip. I stood up and she slapped a cushion over the seat to hide the hole from the audience. It was with great relief that I backed off the stage. The physical pain, coupled with the intimate fumbling I had received, had left me in a bit of a state.

After the show, she and I laughed about it as we sat in the pub in the same corner where we had the long talk about *Hamlet* a few nights before.

Next day in the letter-rack at the stage-door, there was a postcard addressed to me. It was from Annie. It was a photograph of Olivier as Hamlet, which I still have to this day. On the back she had written:

The play's the thing
Wherein I'll catch my doo-dahs on a spring.

*　　*　　*

People, that is to say actors, seemed to come and go quite frequently during these months. Big Annie was snatched from me after only three weeks. We had had such colossal fun together, though the nearest we ever got to being physical was my extrication from the sofa-spring. Hilary Dean left, after having played the lead in *Rebecca*. She looked so like Joan Fontaine that sooner or later it was inevitable. Glenn, playing Maxim de Winter in one of his suave leading-man performances, didn't get many opportunities for jokes in that particular role. I played Giles, and enjoyed myself, doubling with the old boatman, Tabb, who had a broad Cornish accent. I relished anything with an accent, and the audience always loved an actor to play two parts.

The excellent ASM with the personal problem also left, which cleared the air somewhat. A tall, rather grand girl took her place for a few weeks, who was efficient but very distant. So distant now I can't even remember her name.

I was beginning to play larger parts and was glad to. I was learning all the time, especially where comedy was concerned, from Glenn Melvyn. I loved acting with him because, apart from anything else, he was so funny at rehearsals. However, it was an increasing burden to play larger roles and at the same time continue to run the stage-management. But youth was on my side, and I slept well and stayed healthy.

I even decided at one stage to diet from my chubby eleven stone three to a sylph-like ten stone four. I achieved this by eating only tomatoes for lunch and taking a pill which I am not allowed to name within these pages. This drug is now 'prescription only', but then it was freely available. All it did was take away my hunger and if taken after 2 p.m. would keep me awake at night. God knows why I decided to diet at all, bearing in mind that I am now fifteen stone ten and have been sixteen and a half in the heyday of *The Two Ronnies*. It couldn't have been to please some girl, as there was no one around at that particular time. Maybe it was for a particular part I was going to play but I doubt it, for we rarely knew what was coming more than a week or two ahead.

Each month a poster was printed to hang in the shop-windows and suchlike places, advertising the next four plays, and it was then that we found out what was ahead of us. Glenn and I used to see who could make up the best composite title, using bits of all four titles and amalgamating them into one. The best as far as I can remember was during the month when we did *Smiling Through*, *The Corn is Green*, *Ma's Bit of Brass* and *Arsenic and Old Lace*. Glenn won it with 'Smilin' Through the Corn at Ma's Brass Arsenic'.

It was about this time that I was introduced to what were called cue copies. Instead of a full script, each character received a typewritten booklet, usually bound in a sort of brown paper and invariably very tattered and torn. This contained only the last three or four words spoken by the actor before. You can imagine the chaos this caused, as you never knew what was said to you until you heard it at rehearsal and so you listened, desperately hoping to catch the three words you were waiting for, which was your cue to speak. I presume these scripts were produced for the sake of economy, which just shows what a shoe-string these companies operated on. Be that as it may, the muddle this produced was widespread, mainly because although you knew which character gave you your cue, you never knew whether your line followed the first time he or she spoke, or three pages later. If Lady Farnsworth said, '. . . isn't that right?' you spoke your line, because that was the cue for your speech. But it was possible that

Lady Farnsworth was addressing someone else and was not intending to ask your opinion until later in the scene.

We loathed these dreadful little copies when they turned up. Sometimes, because of the fact that they were usually falling to pieces, you would even find pages taped back in the wrong order, which once resulted in Eric, playing a police inspector, denouncing the villainess with the words, 'So you see, Mrs Cavendish, I have definite proof that you murdered your husband *right here in this room*,' only to find that Mrs Cavendish had already made her exit and I, as the old butler, was the only person left on-stage. 'And what is more, madam, you are a master of disguise,' he added with a flourish. This of course was during the first rehearsal; by the time the play got into performance, these mysteries would have been sorted out, although I often think the rehearsals would have entertained the public much more than some of the dreary dramas printed on these cue copies.

Intonations too were sometimes impossible to predict. Not knowing what was coming, you often did not know where the emphasis should come in your line. I once had a line, the cue to which was '. . . strong enough, John?' And my line as John was (indicating barrel), 'Aye. There's some body in that.'

Naturally I thought, before I had heard the full line from the other actor, that I was revealing the location of the man the police were looking for who was hiding inside the barrel, but then I heard the actor say, 'The beer for the outing. Do you think this one is strong enough, John?'

My line was obviously a comment on the quality of the beer. Nevertheless, I couldn't resist at rehearsals saying, 'There's somebody *in* that!' I got my laugh from the cast, but when it came to the performance it was difficult for us to keep straight faces on the stage.

This whole business of inflexion and emphasis on words has always been of great interest and amusement to me. On the printed page, a collection of words in a certain order can sometimes mean more than one thing. If a man says to a girl, in a script, 'I can't leave without making love to you,' and the girl's reply is, 'Why not?' does she fling herself into a recumbent position on the sofa? In this case she says, 'Why not?' meaning, 'Certainly, why not?' However, she may be giving herself to this man contrary to the intentions of the plot. Perhaps she should say 'Why not?' meaning, 'Why can you not leave without making love to me?' If the play is a drama, he might say, 'Because I cannot live without you,' or if it is a farce, 'Because my taxi hasn't arrived.'

Similarly, a police constable talking to Hercule Poirot might say, 'Someone asked me if the butler did it, Monsieur Poirot, and I think he's right.' Poirot replies, 'Who asked you?' Should it be, '*Who* asked you?' (which of the suspects made that enquiry) or 'Who asked *you*?' (you jumped-up little pipsqueak).

These difficulties are soon sorted out because the next line will clarify the meaning, but a similar ambivalence in a story or article in a newspaper remains for ever in doubt.

The Newport bird-fanciers' meeting; prizes awarded were First Prize, Mrs Jennifer Colby (cockatoos). Second, Mrs Arthur Johnson (bullfinches). Third, Mrs Cullimore-Jacobs (fantails). Special mention was made by the chairman of Miss Rose Bulmer's great tits.

You have to laugh, really, don't you?

*   *   *

It was about this time that I struck up a rather odd friendship with a somewhat older woman. When I say older, I mean that I was twenty-one and she was thirty-four, so she was half as old again as I was. In any event, she seemed quite a lot older. Because I was now appearing in bigger and better parts, my face was becoming more known locally, but I could always find sanctuary in the little café above the front of the theatre. I soon got to know the waitress with the large teeth and when I had sorted out the butter situation (mentioned earlier), we got on very amicably. The place only had seats for about twenty people, mostly in twos and fours, but was rarely full. On this particular lunch-time, however, there seemed to be a bit of a crush, due no doubt to the presence of some special delicacy on the menu posted outside the theatre. The only seat available was at the table for two in the corner, which was occupied by a tall woman engrossed in a copy of *Country Life*.

'I don't suppose Mrs Covington would mind you sharing, only she's got fish,' said the waitress in a whisper. She knew my dislike of fish by this time. 'It's plaice though, not smelly,' she added.

We approached Mrs Covington's table. 'Could this gentleman join you?' said the waitress. 'We're a bit up against it today.'

The lady smiled. 'Of course.' I sat. She smiled again. 'You're at the rep aren't you? I never miss a show. I think you're marvellous.' I preened a little. 'All of you,' she said with an embarrassed laugh, 'not just you.'

'Thank you,' I said, un-preening a little.

'But you're the best,' she continued more boldly. By now I didn't know quite where I was in the preening process, so quickly changed the subject to a discussion of the menu.

'The fish is excellent,' she said.

'I don't like fish,' I said.

'Then you'd absolutely hate this one,' she replied and we laughed.

'What's the name of it, Mrs er –'

'Marion,' she said.

'That's a funny name for a fish,' I said and we laughed again.

'Are you as funny off as you are on?' she said.

'Off and on,' I said, and she choked on her fish. I laughed at first but it was a serious choke, and I finished up slapping her on the back, which did the trick eventually.

'I'm so sorry,' she said, 'you caught me unawares. Mind you it was your fault that I choked in the first place. And now you've beaten me black and blue into the bargain.'

We had a pleasant lunch and at the end of it she asked, 'Will you be in here tomorrow?'

'I could be,' I replied with some warmth.

'Lovely. I'll see you here about one.'

Her sly smile as she turned and went down the stairs left me with rather mixed-up feelings. But next day I was there at five to one, with a certain air of expectancy and curiosity as to what would happen next.

After lunch, she asked me back to her house for coffee. So that's what's happening next, I thought. But to a certain extent I was wrong. It turned out that she was a widow and lonely, wanting a kiss and a cuddle but nothing more. Friendship and companionship, she said, couldn't exist between men and women without some sort of physical contact but she was not ready to move it off the sofa and into the bedroom. This suited me fine at the time. I thought her to be much too old for me in terms of any permanent relationship and so it seemed quite sensible to just be 'kissing cousins' as our friends from across the water call it. (The USA, not the Isle of Wight.)

This arrangement, and indeed our relationship, changed subtly on the arrival of Mandy Kaye in the company.

Mandy arrived to take the place of the distant girl with the forgotten name and of course we were thrown together (in the course of our work) almost at once. A blonde girl with a *retroussé* nose and a rather worldly-wise approach; it might now be called street-wise but in those days didn't just cover the street but seemingly the whole world. It wasn't long before we got so friendly that we were looking for a nice quiet room to express our friendliness in. I had already introduced her to Marion. It was she who suggested that we use her house.

'You can be as friendly as you like,' she said. 'I think young love is wonderful.'

And so it was arranged that Mandy and I would spend afternoons in Marion's bedroom as and when we felt like it, which in the event turned out to be every afternoon. Having, that is, got over the first visit. The whole thing was almost a non-starter from the word go. Having taken tea with Marion in the sitting-room, we both decided that it was time to go into the bedroom to be friendly. As we leapt into bed, naked and reasonably unashamed, Mandy drew the bedclothes up around us and then, in a sort of delayed double-take, threw them back again and looking down at me, exclaimed: 'I thought so!'

'What?' I said, puzzled.

'You're not circumcised!'

'Should I be?'

'Yes! You're Jewish, aren't you?'

'No.'

'But you look Jewish!'

I suppose I did. Dark, with the nose. 'Does it matter?'

'I only sleep with Jewish boys.'

'Why?'

'Because I'm Jewish.' She didn't look Jewish. Blonde, with no nose. I said as much.

'Not *all* Jewish girls are dark with big noses.'

'Not all gentile boys are blond with little noses,' I countered. 'So what are we going to do about it?'

She looked at me and grabbed my nose and other parts of my non-Jewishness. 'There's always a first time, I suppose,' she giggled.

Marion, of course, was delighted when we told her the story and laughed immoderately. From then on she took to bringing us tea and cakes in bed without bothering to knock, even coming in one day as I was chasing Mandy round the bedroom (the reason escapes me), saying, 'I heard all the noise and thought I'd come and see the fun.'

We both had to try to act in an uninhibited manner but Mandy later said she couldn't be doing with that sort of thing.

'What does she think I am? It's not Madame Tussaud's, is it?'

'No,' I said, 'the dummies in there would never be allowed to move like you,' which earned me a swift kick in the gentiles.

Mandy and I worked well as a team in the theatre and we bowed gracefully out of Marion's life in her big house. She didn't seem offended and we would often get a wave from her in the café or from across the street, but nothing more.

Mandy moved her digs. 'She's a fearsome landlady – would never allow a man anywhere near the house after the show.'

'Well, what's the point of that?' I grumbled.

'The point of that is, she works all day until six.'
Nobody's fool was Mandy.

So afternoons we spent for the most part in the pursuit
of love and nights singing in the pub or with Glenn in his
little car. Which only left the actual performance of the
current play to pass the time happily between. It sounds
idyllic and I think for the most part was. I can recall
no disaster or tragedy taking place during those happy
youthful months.

9

There soon followed quite a shake-up in the company. John Pickering-Cail and his wife, Zelda, left to run another company for 'Forty', the boss. Glenn was made Director, which was marvellous and a new chap, Robin McIntyre, arrived to make up the numbers. Robin was an ash-blond Nordic type who was as English as roast beef. He and his fiancée Lorna (the girl that he lived with) were in Forty's company at, I think, Wilmslow, but she had to stay behind, being a great attraction in the company, so she and Robin were parted. Only as far as work was concerned, however, as he would travel back each night by bus and train to his beloved. He was a snooker player too and so we became lunch-time partners. I enjoyed the game enormously and had improved a lot. Glenn, of course, had more work to do now that he was Director, so we saw less of each other socially but more professionally, although we still had our harmony sessions in the car at night, having taken Robin to his bus.

It was Robin who first introduced me to Chinese food. He suggested that we should go to Manchester one Sunday to meet his Lorna and have a meal. 'Do you like Chinese?' he asked me one evening.

'Bit frightening,' I said.

'Frightening, why?'

'There are so many of them.' Being obtuse is often a good way of getting laughs.

'Silly bugger,' said Robin. 'Food, you twit.'

'I knew what you meant,' I said. 'Actually I've never tried it. It's all prawns, isn't it? I don't like fish.'

But it wasn't all prawns I was told and that Sunday we gathered, he, Lorna and I, at the Chinese restaurant.

Lorna was stunning. Violently red hair, pale skin, wonderful cheekbones. I fell instantly in love, but contented myself to worship her from afar, in deference to Robin. They were obviously in love, anyway.

My first experience of Chinese food was a delight, apart from the chopsticks which I instantly thought were silly and the most badly designed object for picking up food ever known. Would anyone seriously suggest that one should eat green peas with knitting needles? Or soup with a fork? Considering the Chinese are such an ancient, cultured and artistic people it makes one wonder how they came up with a real bummer like chopsticks. I went straight for a spoon.

We would often go to Manchester on Sundays after that and always had a great time. I took Mandy, and she and Lorna got on well. Too much lager was drunk, of course, and the train home with Mandy was a rather hazy affair. Not much fun being at the theatre by eight next morning to put up the set. But Frank, the toothless electrician, would be there, bright and early. 'Have a good day off did you?' he would say. 'You look as if you did.'

I would give him a bleary-eyed nod and get stuck into the scenery-shifting.

The sets came from a central store in Manchester which served all of Fortescue's various companies dotted around the area. Sometimes you would get a newly painted set of 'flats', but more often one that had seen a lot of use. There were no facilities for flying the scenery upwards on a pulley, as is usual in most custom-built theatres. This, being a cinema, had no such luxury. So if the set had to be changed during performance, it was manhandled off and on by stage-hands. In our company, there was Daft Tommy (we didn't call him that), Glenn and me. You have to learn to fix the tops together (often twelve feet high) by lassoing a small cleat at the top with the rope attached to the adjoining top. Glenn was an expert, with a deft flick of the wrist and a tug downwards. I practised for hours on end and soon got good at it, so that Glenn and I made a formidable team during quick changes.

We needed all our skills for the play, *Harvey*. Glenn was playing Elwood P Dowd, the man whose constant companion is a six-foot invisible rabbit. Of course everybody thinks he is two sandwiches short of a picnic, but he himself knows the rabbit is real. A great comedy, but one which requires nine changes of scenery each performance. Only two sets – but one is set inside the other, then taken away, then set again etc etc etc, nine times a show.

On August Bank Holiday we did three shows. Approaching the end of the third one, I, who only appeared in one five-minute scene as a negro cab-driver, was exhausted. Glenn, virtually never off the stage during the entire performance, was like a rag. We had changed the set twenty-six times that day. He and I stared at each other in a stupor.

'It's no good giving me that black look,' said Glenn to my negro make-up. 'I'm playing the bloody lead as well.'

At that point our cue came to enter together. Glenn opened the door as I was carrying his suitcases. We walked through the door and straight into the back of the other set. In our exhaustion we had waited outside the main set door instead of the inner set door. There was a foot to spare between the two sets, so we crashed our way round, me with two suitcases, and entered, stifling giggles, to an audience bewildered by the shaking and banging of the set. Glenn bowed to the actress already on-stage and said, 'Sorry to be a trifle delayed, ma'am, but there's a herd of cattle in the outer office.'

This of course did nothing to help me control my fit of giggles, and afterwards, when we came off, I said, 'Sorry I laughed, but it was practically impossible to get round with those two suitcases.'

'How do you think *I* felt,' said Glenn, 'I had a flaming six-foot rabbit with me.'

I slept like a baby that night after probably the hardest day's work I ever did at Bramhall.

I suppose when I think about it that exhaustion was always just around the corner. It was a terribly energy-consuming job. The constant strain of appearing at one's very best each night except Sunday, week after week, needed a pretty cast-iron constitution. It also needed youth, I believe. Those older members of the company must have been drained of energy every night, only to drag themselves back in the morning to test their memories on the next play. Remember, they had to learn forty minutes of lines a day.

Tiredness and tension showed itself in many ways. One of the worst was what we called looping the loop. This consisted in missing out a piece of script which contained plot and 'jumping' to a page or so later. Upon realising this, the actor would endeavour to put back the missing piece of script so as not to lose the audience, who were desperately trying to keep up (especially in Agatha Christie). He would then be terrified of looping the loop, that is to say repeating the bit he had already said. Are you with me so far? Because he must now jump that bit as well and try to remember at what point he must resume the script – making sure not to repeat anything but again not leaving a bit out.

I can quite understand you not following all that at first reading, but the actor had to. He must do all the above in order to restore the plot and the play to an even keel. All this, while at the same time saying the lines and giving a performance. What a nightmare! This same tiredness, coupled with the fact that the words, especially on first nights, are still fairly unfamiliar, can cause mistakes which can be disastrous to the story, or hilarious to the rest of the cast depending on how they manifest themselves. If the wrong name is used in a murder mystery for instance, it could make nonsense of the plot. Juxtaposition of words can make a dramatic line ridiculous.

In Somerset Maugham's *The Letter*, the lawyer is supposed to say to the leading lady, 'Pull yourself together, madam, you are going to pieces.' Instead, at this most dramatic moment in the play, he grabbed her by the shoulders and shouted, 'Pull yourself to pieces, madam!' The actor making this sort of gaffe then has to decide whether to carry on and ignore it, or go back and correct it. It often seems safer to leave well alone.

A leading lady at Bramhall in a rather turgid play about a family firm in financial difficulties, had the difficult task of coping with a lot of technical business jargon and so was always rather rocky on the lines. She had to say to me, playing the younger brother, 'Any breath of scandal would put me in bad odour with the board. I would be, in their eyes, pretty petty.' Instead she heard herself saying, 'Any odour of scandal would put me in bad breath with the board.' I controlled myself and saw her eyes flicker, deciding to go on rather than back. She continued the speech. 'I would pee,' she said, and we both instantly turned upstage to hide our faces. She gave up completely on that line and waited for me to say my next line, which I did as soon as I could gain control of my features. She and I had a good laugh about it later, of course.

She was a great girl, with the unlikely name of Patricia Pilkington and had arrived after Zelda left. She obviously didn't think too much of her name either, because she changed it to Phoenix and shortened Patricia to Pat. Then she proceeded to become a household name in *Coronation Street*.

Because I have no written record or diaries of this period and am relying completely on memory, I have no idea when events took place. Nor did I notice the weather or the seasons of the year, but I look back on this time as generally pleasant and sunny. By now I suppose the leaves must have fallen and Christmas was approaching. I now have to confess that I cannot remember anything about the Christmas production or indeed Christmas itself.

In my property-book, which I still have, with details of props and when to set and strike them – my bible during the evening performance – there are details of a production called *The Magic Cracker* sandwiched between *Lover's Leap* and *Little Women*. It took place in five scenes, so the book says, and among the characters were 'Mr Twinkle (dame), Miss Pidgeon (Baroness), Tina (Prince) and Elf' so there was obviously a plot in which ordinary people became pantomime characters. Miss Pidgeon had cough sweets in the first act and mention is also made of paper snow, boxes of crackers, a moon which descended from the 'skies' above (together with some five-pound notes) and directions for the placing of the 'flashes', made of magnesium, and the smoke pellets which would be triggered electronically at various positions on the stage. Not much fun if you forget where they are and are standing over one when it goes off. In the panto at Aylesbury, one of the dancing 'babes', all about fourteen years old, stood uncomfortably close to a flash when it was ignited, though luckily not completely over it. The girl escaped injury, but her knickers were a write-off.

There was, I see, a 'troupe' in this show, because there is a direction to set their tap mats ready for scene five. This troupe of young ladies would no doubt be from the local dancing school and would have been on the whole perfect pests, with a chaperone herding them up like a mother hen and shepherding them back to their dressing-room after each appearance.

All this information comes from my prop-book but I have absolutely no recollection of the piece at all. I remember people and incidents much more clearly than the content of the various plays we were performing each week. These were merely a backdrop to the characters and events; they didn't themselves register in my memory. This is probably because it was always necessary to forget completely last week's play in order to make room for this week's and next week's pieces. Previous lines must be completely erased from the brain and this was a natural process, one's memory simply letting go of them and allowing them to slip away.

The most common question asked of an actor by a member of the public is, 'How do you perform one and learn another at the same time without getting mixed up?' The answer has to be, 'I don't know, it just never happens.' And so plays are generally lost to me but people remain. I remember Robin so clearly although I cannot see him playing any one particular character. I remember us both sitting up all night with a bottle of gin on the eve of my birthday, in a cottage that we had been lent for the week by some affluent acquaintance. At dawn, we ran down to a stream at the bottom of the garden to watch the sun come up over the water-meadows. I remember it so very clearly. What I don't remember is the colossal hangover we must have taken into rehearsals, some three hours later. But then, who wants to remember a hangover?

I think Robin and I did quite a lot of drinking. We were both the sort of people who got very happy and euphoric after partaking of the demon, full of plans for the future, opening our own repertory company, staging a tour and so on. Robin was also one to do things on the spur of the moment and I, being then in the same state of mind, would almost always fall in with his plans as we fell out of the pub.

At this point I should say that the theatrical landlady is for the most part a treasure and much care had to be taken to cherish her friendship and surrogate-mother affection. So when Mrs Holmes, my landlady, suggested that Robin should come back to supper I readily agreed. 'He can stay the night in the spare room,' she said benignly, albeit asthmatically. 'I shall be in bed, so don't make too much racket.'

Robin welcomed the idea (Lorna, his girl, was away) and we went to the pub as usual for a jar or three before going back. We were doing a short play that week, so more time for last orders. Shortly after we arrived, Glenn and his wife Joan breezed in and we formed a melodic foursome in the corner. Several halves later, Robin was suddenly consumed with a desire for a Chinese meal. 'Alcohol creates in me a craving for the exotic,' he announced somewhat poetically. Glenn immediately suggested we drive into Manchester (he was the one with the car) and we all chorused agreement loud and clear. So loud and clear that the landlord shouted, 'Hey, shut up, you noisy buggers! Haven't you got no pissing homes to go to?' Another with a poetic turn of phrase.

A splendid, enormous meal was had by all, Robin caught his last train, and Glenn and Joan dropped me off at about one in the morning. I crept in and made for the stairs. As I did so I glanced through the open door into the dining-room. My heart sank. How could I have completely forgotten? An enormous meal lay on the table. Gigantic ham salads for two. Bread and butter and a two-tiered dish of fancy cakes.

There was only one thing to be done. Having had a very hefty Chinese meal and several (at least) beers, I sat down at one in the morning and ate both salads and two of the fancy cakes. And in case Mrs Holmes was lying awake upstairs, I kept up a low murmur of conversation with myself. Afterwards I opened the front door, said, 'Goodnight, Robin' to an empty street, closed the door and dragged myself heavily to bed.

Landladies, you see, must be humoured and looked after, if you want them to look after you. That is why they always received two tickets for Monday night's show, free of charge. Most of them too were never backward in coming forward with hints, suggestions and criticisms of the play or the performances. I once had a landlady say to me, 'You're always different, every week, aren't you?'

'I try to be,' I replied.

'Yes,' she said, 'I like that John, he's a good actor. No matter what sort of part he's playing, he's always the same.'

Her friend who always accompanied her said on another occasion, 'You do very good make-ups, being all these different people. You take a lot of trouble. I always know it's you, though.'

Eccentric, too, most of them. One large woman would come alone, using the other free seat to put her coat and hat on. She would sit in the front row of the stalls and knit, all through the performance. She knitted very fast.

'Why does she knit so fast?' I said to Glenn during the first interval one Monday night. In the second interval, having had time to think about it, he said, 'I think it's because she's trying to finish that jumper before the wool runs out.' A nonsensical, sideways sort of humour he had. So many gems!

Some landladies, of course, would go too far, either in the way of meanness, or lack of services, or simply downright rudeness to their lodgers. Glenn was full of landlady stories. 'I once complained to one old bag about there being no back-scrubbing brush in the bathroom. She said, "Well, you've got a tongue in your head, haven't you?" and I said, "What do you think I am, a bloody contortionist?"'

The classic retribution was, so I'm told, to nail a kipper underneath the dining-table just before you left on the Sunday. After a week or so, the stench would be frightful and no one could find it.

10

Shortly after the salad incident, I took on a new landlady. I cannot remember why I left Mrs Holmes but it must have been to do with her health. I think, being asthmatic and it must be said very overweight, she decided she must call it a day and bring her career as a landlady to the Thespians of this parish to an end. She gave me plenty of notice, which enabled me to put the word about in the pub that I was seeking accommodation.

I didn't have to put it about very far. In fact, I turned to the chap next to me and said, 'I'm looking for a room,' and he said 'I've got one you can have.' I knew the man – let's call him Charlie – and I knew where he lived. He and his wife ran a little grocer's shop (with house attached) about half a mile from the theatre. To cut a short story even shorter, I accepted and moved in the following Sunday.

He was a nice, whimsical fellow who drove a contraption called a Bond Minicar. This name might create an image of Ian Fleming's 007 character and it was indeed a rather outlandish sort of vehicle, rather narrower at the front end, giving it the appearance of a flying corned-beef tin. It had only three wheels and probably about two horsepower (one of them on its last legs). It could carry a passenger, but you sort of slid into it and lay there as if in some sort of space module. When in motion, your backside was so close to the ground that if you went over cat's eyes, you knew it. Luckily in those days there were no such things as 'sleeping policemen' because going over one of those would have amounted to indecent assault. The vehicle had one advantage over other cars. If you parked it badly in front of other cars, it could be lifted out of the way.

My bedroom over the back storeroom of the shop was very comfortable, with a sitting area, desk and swivel chair where I could make out my prop and furniture lists, and a window looking out onto the vegetable garden. It was known at the time in theatrical parlance as a 'combined chat', but don't ask me why. I liked the swivel chair. It reminded me of all those detective novels I used to read.

There was a knock at the door. Philip swivelled round to face it. 'You!' he cried. 'No,' she said. 'It's not her, it's me.' She closed the door, unable to look at him. 'Clancy's dead,' he said suddenly. She swivelled round to face him.

She had obviously brought her own swivel chair with her. Mine was brown leather, cracked and chewed in places, but very comfortable. I took to it at once.

I moved in on the Sunday morning, accompanied by the church bells, and by the evening had got myself organised. I was sitting at my desk, looking out of the window and thinking how comfortable everything seemed, when there was a tap on the door. I swivelled round and said 'Come in.' (This was, in fact, my very first swivel, and I enjoyed it.) My new landlady was a pleasant, comfortable lady with flyaway spectacles and the suspicion of a tint about her sandy hair. She had come to tell me that she didn't think she could run to breakfast in the kitchen each day. 'Too chaotic in the mornings, love, but Dulcie will come up and wake you if that's all right.'

'Who's Dulcie?' I enquired, having visions of Dulcie turning out to be a great big St Bernard dog leaping on the bed at eight o'clock every morning.

'Dulcie works in the shop. I'm training her. She's ever so nice. She'll bring up your breakfast. OK?'

Dulcie was indeed ever so nice. At sixteen years old, she was the sweetest, plumpest, prettiest country girl you could imagine, with the rosy bloom of peaches in her cheeks and the thickest accent in the neighbourhood. She was a darling. Each morning she would bring my breakfast, and open the curtains, and tell me not to go to sleep again, else my tea would get cold. What a charming start to the day, I would think, as I munched and slurped my solitary toast and tea.

In spite of the faint odour she would leave behind of paraffin, Sunlight soap and dog biscuits from the shop below, the lasting impression of her was sweetness and light. My thoughts at that time never went further, because Mandy was still the girl in my life.

But not for much longer. She had had a good deal of experience before she came to Bramhall, in acting as well as without doubt in life, love and the pursuit of happiness. One of her earlier boyfriends wrote to her, offering her a very good part in a long national tour he was directing, and she accepted. We parted, tearful, but with no regrets. We had both enjoyed each other so much; how could there be regrets? She went and I missed her for a long time to come.

But there was continually so much work to be done, so many plays to get on by Monday and off by Saturday, and each day was crammed full of activity and incident. I was enjoying Glenn's direction, always constructive and often very innovative in spite of the very short time available for rehearsal. He was so entertaining off-stage, full of stories of his earliest days in 'fit-up', one-night stands in outlandish places, and of the tragi-comic personalities who inhabited these often very shoddy companies.

He told me of a very young lad in his first speaking part on the boards who was so petrified that before the curtain rose on the first night, he dropped to his knees in the wings and began to pray to his Maker. He felt a tap on the shoulder. He looked round to see the imposing, cloaked figure of the leading man. 'Don't rely on him too much in the third act, laddie, he's helping me with a quick change.'

Charlie, my new landlord, he of the flying corned-beef tin, was also of a droll and comical nature. Indeed, it seemed that it was (and I'm sure still is) a very important part of the Northerner's daily life, this business of making the other chap laugh. In the snooker room at the Victoria Arms, the straight-faced jokes were constantly on the boil.

'Weather's very changeable,' I remarked to an old boy in the corner. The answer came straight back.

'I know. Just lately we haven't had a single day alike.'

Their timing always seemed immaculate. It was Charlie who taught me a comical little stanza that I shall always remember. It's almost impossible to indicate comedy timing on paper, but if you imagine a tiny pause at the end of each line, and the last line flowing through, spoken in an imploring tone, then it may work.

Don't mind me daughter, sir,
She can't hold her water, sir,
Everytime she laughs, she pees.
Look, there she goes, sir, all down her clothes, sir, don't
make her laugh, sir, please.

I was so tickled with this piece of nonsense and the way it was performed that I couldn't wait to tell Robin, who loved it just as much as I did. A week or so later I was playing a country squire in one of those plays with the cue scripts. My line (to Robin as a young buck) was, 'Pay no heed to Melissa, sir, she is too young to know her own mind.' Of course, what I said to Robin was, 'Don't mind me daughter, sir, she's too young to know her own mind.' Needless to say, he got a very bad coughing fit before I had finished the line. In fact, he began to make choking noises, so I grabbed the carafe from the table, saying, 'Do have some water, sir,' which made it worse. He did drink some water, but a new wave of laughter came over him. The result was his mouthful of water finished up on my waistcoat. All in all, we were both in a state by the time we got off-stage.

Glenn was in the wings. He was furious and told us so in no uncertain terms. He was the first person to enjoy a joke on-stage, but he was a hard taskmaster and quite rightly, when we allowed things to get out of control. His first thoughts were always for the audience, the people who put the wages into our pockets. 'They are the only people who matter,' was his maxim. Efficiency was his watchword in every facet of the rehearsals and performances that came and went with such rapidity, and to this day this has always been my goal. I know that in later years, when more in control of what I did and performed, I was regarded by many as pernickety, fussing about detail, but to me it was just getting it right, as right as it was possible to get it. Glenn taught me that and I'm grateful that he did.

He regarded me as efficient even then, in fact so much so that one day he called me into his dressing-room and said, 'Ron, old son, I've been thinking about your future.

You're such a damned good Stage Manager. Your acting's OK, but your real strength lies in your organising ability. Now, as you know, the job of Company Manager with Frank Fortescue involves directing and keeping the books and, of course, overseeing the stage-management. That's what I'm doing at the moment. I could speak to Forty, he trusts my word. He would give you a job as Company Manager like a shot. And the point is, you could be earning twenty pounds a week in a year or two. What d'you think?'

I reacted immediately. 'Would I be allowed to act, as you are at present?'

'No,' said Glenn, 'I'm only managing the company temporarily, until we get a new man. No, Forty doesn't like his managers performing.'

My next question was obvious. 'Would *you* give up acting to be a manager?'

'No, I'm afraid I wouldn't.'

'Thank God for that,' I said, 'and neither will I.' He laughed.

'Well, don't blame me if you're out of work for half your life. Acting means that much to you, does it?'

I said it did.

'Well, maybe you'll get lucky. Shouldn't you be calling the half?'

I rushed away without even looking at my watch and knocked on all the doors. 'Half an hour, please.'

As I got back to Glenn's door, I shouted, 'I'm not as efficient as all that, I nearly missed it.'

'No, you're not.' He put his head round his dressing-room door. 'There's nearly an hour to go yet,' and, ducking, rushed inside and bolted the door. I loved the man.

* * *

I was thoroughly enjoying myself at Bramhall, but I missed Oxford. Although not actually born there, I regarded it as my home town, having lived there since I was four years old and having been to school there – not only infant, junior and grammar school, but also for a brief five months as a student of architecture. Thank God that didn't work out, otherwise I would have missed so much fun in my life. But Oxford as it was then, before it had the middle ripped out of it to build a shopping centre, was an enchanting place. All the roads were two-way for a start and although I only aspired to a bicycle, the freedom to roam up The High, down St Giles' or St Aldate's, across Port Meadow, or along the towpath from Folly Bridge to Iffley Lock, was a joy and a memory that the years cannot dim. This longing developed into acute home-sickness when I received a letter from Ivor Humphris, an old chum from amateur drama days. He and Mike Ford, the third member of our erstwhile trio were both, he informed me, now working at the Playhouse!

Oxford Playhouse had been my Mecca since the moment I became a professional actor. I had seen so many marvellous productions there, often starring John Moffatt or Patricia Gilder. I still have their autographs, written in Patricia's eyebrow pencil, when I met them as an ardent schoolboy fan at the great annual St Giles' fair. The Playhouse was the place I took a girl on my very first date, complete with small box of Cadbury's Milk Tray and enough money for two back-row tickets, two ice creams and the bus fare home.

What were these two chaps doing there working, albeit backstage, without me? I wrote back to Ivor, expressing my indignation, but got a reply instead from Mike Ford. 'Why don't you write to Frank Shelley? I'll mention you to him.' Frank Shelley was God at Oxford Playhouse. Was it remotely possible that the lowly technician who was in charge of the music had the temerity to deliver a petition to the feet of the Master? Apparently he had, and apparently he did.

'Let me know when you can get down,' he wrote again, 'and Frank says he will arrange to see you.'

I shook with nerves as I approached Glenn. My plan was not to mention this correspondence, but to tackle it in a more roundabout way.

'Any chance of a week out, Glenn?' I enquired with a pathetic attempt at nonchalance. 'I'd like to get home, see the folks.'

Glenn suspected nothing. After all, a lad of twenty-one could be forgiven for a little home-sickness.

'Can't be next week, there's a good part for you next week. Funny. How about the week after?'

I think I should explain here that one week out is, as far as appearing in a play is concerned, more than one week. If you work in a bank, you simply go away for one week and return on the following Monday. A 'week out' in a play is more complicated. Week one, you perform at night but don't rehearse because you won't be there next week. Week two, you are away, so do not appear or rehearse. Week three, you return and rehearse but do not appear as you weren't there last week to rehearse! So, in effect, you miss two plays.

So it took a total of three weeks before I got back to dear old Oxford. I arrived on Sunday afternoon, ready for my interview with the Almighty on the following morning. I shook as I entered Frank's office, the inner sanctum, the holy of holies.

Frank Shelley turned out to be charming. His booming voice shook the glass in a bookcase when he reached certain registers but his charisma was very strong. Remember, I had seen him give many great performances in the past, so there was a star-struck quality in my attitude which he may or may not have noticed.

'The first thing I have to tell you,' he boomed, rattling the bookcase, 'is that I have no acting jobs.' Despair. 'But I could do with another person on publicity. How would you feel about that?'

My brain raced. Get in, doesn't matter how. Acting will come later, with luck. 'Yes, I'd like that.'

'Have you ever done publicity?'

'Yes, some.' This was almost a lie – I had handed out leaflets at Aylesbury.

'Good.' He slid back the glass on the bookshelves and took out a folder. 'This will tell you about what I'm doing at the moment. Publicity-wise,' he boomed. The bookcase glass, now in a different position, vibrated even more as he spoke. 'Damned glass,' he said, 'traffic vibration,' and he gave it a tap with his foot.

There was a knock at the door and a lady bearing two cups of coffee entered. 'Thanks, Cynthia. Cynthia, this is Mr Baker.'

'Barker,' I corrected.

'Yes, whatever,' he replied. She smiled and left. 'Now, what I want you to do is this. Get yourself a notebook, have a look round the theatre, and if you can come up with three good ideas and tell them to me tomorrow at eleven, I'll take you on.' The two cups of coffee had now joined the glass bookcase in a concerted rattle, almost drowning my acceptance of the challenge.

I was allowed to wander round the Playhouse; the auditorium dark and quiet like any other auditorium. The coffee bar upstairs, open to the public, in which sat groups of university students, mostly on the floor, to the obvious displeasure of the lady of uncertain years who ran the place.

'Mind your cigarette, Sonny Jim,' she snapped at me as she passed. I flicked my lengthening ash into the saucer of a nearby used coffee-cup – the ashtrays all being on the floor in the midst of the students – and stared at the bare walls of the bar. Posters, photos, forthcoming production notices all over these for a start, I thought. I passed by Frank's office as I descended the stairs to the street. Frank was on the phone. His doorknob was vibrating like a thing demented.

When I returned the next morning at eleven, I had ten or a dozen ideas in my notebook. Frank read them in silence. Nothing in the room rattled. Eventually he spoke.

'Excellent!' he cried and the room burst into vibrant life again. I noticed a new participant, a glass standing alongside a whisky bottle on the top of the bookcase. 'OK, you get the job. Now, money. What were you getting at Bromley?'

'Bramhall,' I said.

'Yes, whatever.'

'Eight pounds a week,' I lied. I was getting six.

'Impossible to pay you that. I'll give you three.'

The room suddenly went quiet as if waiting for my answer.

'It's a big drop. If I was satisfactory, could you put it up to five in, say, a month?'

'Why not, why not?' came the reply, and the room rattled its relief.

So I was in. Now all I had to do was to break the news to Glenn. I travelled back to Bramhall after a week at home, a week of euphoria spent with my old friends Ivor and Mike and of course my mother and father. Mother especially was overjoyed that I would be back living at home, as indeed was I.

But back to Bramhall and two final weeks of performing before changing course and becoming an ad-man. This was the most difficult thing of all to say to Glenn, that I was giving up acting.

'You told me you couldn't ever do that a week or two ago,' he complained. I told him of my hopes, that sooner or later I would get my foot in the acting door at Oxford. 'Well, let's hope so, old son. We shall miss you. *I* shall miss you. Still, two weeks' notice to serve here yet.'

And so began a series of lengthy goodbyes to the people with whom I had become involved during my year's stay. To the furniture shop in Charlton and Mr Crossdale.

'We never did get that stuffed crocodile on the set, did we?' he said. 'What a monster. I don't know why anyone should want to stuff a crocodile in the first place. Must have been done for a joke.'

'Aye, stuff that for a lark,' I said. He laughed and I realised that in the short time I had been up in Cheshire, I had picked up the Northern way of speaking. I said 'Aye' instead of 'Yes'. I said 'Give us a lift' instead of 'Give me a hand'. And I had developed a bit of an accent too, I was told when I returned to Oxford during that week.

I said goodbye to Mrs Barraclough, just round the corner from the theatre, who had often given me cups of tea while I chose bric-à-brac for the set from her little shop.

'I'm not going to stick it much longer myself,' she said. 'My hubby wants me to stop. He doesn't agree with women working. Whenever he sees me in the garden chopping wood, it upsets him so, he can't watch and has to go indoors.'

She, like the others, had this droll sense of the ridiculous. My landlady and landlord too said they would be sorry to lose me. And, of course, Dulcie, the girl who brought my breakfast, expressed great sadness. 'I shall miss you ever so much,' she said in her thick-as-two-slices accent.

I had been getting on very well with Dulcie. Each morning she would wake me with my breakfast and a smile. One morning she was looking so adorable, I said, 'Don't I get a good morning kiss, then?' She leaned over the bed, kissed me lightly on the lips, blushed and left the room quickly. It became a morning ritual, the kisses getting longer and less embarrassed. I took to grabbing her and giving her a cuddle sometimes, to which she would react anxiously, saying, 'Hey up, give over, Missus will hear us. You've got no clothes on!' So I was forced to behave, but we both enjoyed the clandestine kiss each morning.

My last night at the theatre arrived all too soon. The play was *Too Young to Marry* in which Glenn and I had had a great deal of fun during the week's run. On the Saturday night at the curtain call, Glenn made the usual speech thanking the audience for being 'wonderful'. They were always 'wonderful' in the curtain-call speech, whatever they had been like. He then told the audience that I was leaving, and made me take a bow on my own. A sad, sad moment, with the cast as well as the audience applauding me. During this applause, Glenn left the stage and returned with a brand-new shiny metal case containing a billiard-cue. The audience as well as the cast knew of my liking for the game and a roar of approval went up as I accepted it as a leaving present from the cast and backstage staff. Lengthy emotional goodbyes followed after the curtain fell and continued in my under-stage dressing-room accompanied by beer and wine out of prop glasses. The man who was taking over as Stage Manager was there too.

In Oxford as a lad, I had been a member of the St James Church choir. The head choirboy was Victor Grant and we had never got on very well. He was, I thought at the time, far too snobbish and self-important. The long arm of coincidence has to me never been more stretched than when, in Bramhall, in the foyer of the theatre, I met the man who was to succeed me. It was Victor Grant. He was naturally as surprised as I was and during the week, showing him the ropes, I realised that he was a perfectly pleasant chap, with no more snobbish 'side'. One of us had changed, either him or me.

But the backstage party was ended; fond farewells were made, amid kisses and hugs. I rose next morning with the Sunday church bells ringing in my ears, not helping my hangover one bit. I had originally intended to travel back to Oxford that day, but two things changed my mind. One, the Sunday trains were hopeless, with long waits between changes. Two, I had a date with Dulcie.

I had taken advantage of her obvious regret that I would soon be leaving by suggesting that she and I might go out together one evening. She seemed very keen on the idea, but couldn't on the first Sunday as she was going out with her parents. It had to be a Sunday because I was working every evening during the week, so the only day left was that final Sunday before my departure.

I had found out that she had no regular boyfriend, so I felt I was not treading on anybody's toes. She was so desirable and only sixteen years old. 'I'll be seventeen in August,' she had said, like an eager child wishing all the time to be older. She was, of course, still almost a child, but as I packed my belongings that afternoon I couldn't help thinking of what might transpire that night. I would have to tread carefully, but I was determined to do my best to talk her round and, to use the most polite expression I can think of, 'make her mine'.

The time came to pick her up at her house. I arrived on time, and she appeared in a most pretty pink dress, with a full skirt and a low-cut bodice. I thought to myself, well, everything looks to be fully get-at-able, and immediately thought, don't be disgusting, what a thing to think about such a pretty dress. But think it I did, I have to confess.

She seemed happy and relaxed, and we went to the pub as arranged. A country inn, half a mile's walk from her house, through country lanes and across a small common. There were kisses on the way but only as a sort of curtain-raiser to the main event. In the pub she didn't drink much. A rum and 'pep', and two lemonades. I drank three halves of bitter. Crisps, peanuts and cheese biscuits in packets were our supper that evening, in those days before the advent of the ploughman's platter or the microwaved pizza.

It was a warm spring night when we left the pub and found a quiet spot on the lane for a bit of serious canoodling. She was so sweet to kiss and made no objection to my fondling, once I had found my way in through the pretty frills which covered her bosom. Her kisses got more ardent and my hands wandered lower, negotiating the skirt. Suddenly she stopped me.

'No, Ron, I can't let you. I'm sorry, I can't.'

'Have you not, well, like, done it before?' I whispered. Even as I said it, I realised that I was being too forward, too persuasive, to a young girl of such tender years. Naturally, she was virginal; whatever made me think she wasn't? 'I'm sorry. I didn't realise you hadn't done it before.'

She drew back a little. 'Who, me?' she said. 'I love it. I do it all the time.'

'Then why –'

She kissed me, long and hard. 'It's the wrong time of the month,' she said.

Next morning, on the train home, thinking about the whole incident, of all the earlier wasted opportunities with this little sexpot, I was reflecting on the ironies of life as I watched the cows and sheep flying past the window. The middle-aged woman opposite me asked if she could borrow my newspaper. 'I follow the stars,' she said.

'Stage and screen?' I suggested.

'No, *astrology*,' she replied rather reprovingly. 'What sign are you? When were you born?'

I told her, 25th September. 'Virgo, aren't I?' I said.

'Virgo? No, no, you're not a Virgo. It's the wrong time of the month.'

'You're the second woman to say that to me in twenty-four hours.'

11

Oxford. City of dreaming spires and lost bicycles. My home town, my home repertory company, my local and well-beloved theatre. The place where I had dreamed my way through so many wonderful productions in earlier times, dreaming that I too might one day tread the boards on the other side of the footlights. My Mecca. Now my dreams were to be realised. My day-to-day life took on a magic quality.

Of course, my dreams were at first only partly come true, only semi-realised. Because I was the man who took round the handbills to the shops, not the man who cavorted on the stage. I was the chap who, armed with a bundle of 'throwaways' advertising forthcoming productions, wandered round the town trying to get rid of them wherever I could: in bicycle baskets, behind windscreen wipers, under milk bottles and even, in desperation, tucked in between the leaflets at the Ashmolean Museum, in the racks saying 'please take one'.

'I'm very keen on publicity,' Frank Shelley had declaimed, his voice dislodging a piece of plaster from the ceiling. 'Nothing is too much trouble.'

He certainly kept us at it. Duncan, who was head of publicity and whose entourage consisted of myself and

Bert Lyon (a lanky cockney lightning cartoonist of some fifty summers whom Frank had met up with and put on the payroll), would sit with us in his little office, trying to think of ways of advertising. We came up with book-matches and window displays which I, having been to an architectural school, was considered best qualified to design and make. Ideas which were either discarded or ruled out by Frank included cloth banners on the sides of Salters' Steamers on the river and toilet paper bearing the message *Now wash your hands and afterwards visit The Playhouse Theatre.* The banners were considered expensive and the toilet paper discarded on grounds of taste, 'because,' said Frank, 'you never know where it will end up.' I argued that, on the contrary, we all had a pretty good idea where it would end up but was overruled.

In the main, however, the work consisted in slogging round with posters, handbills and throwaways. I would, of course, sneak in and watch rehearsals when I could and also, because I was intrigued, visit the scenedock where a fascinating man called Paul Mayo would be practising his art as designer and painter of the sets. He looked exactly like Paul Scofield; in fact, he once sat next to him in the milk bar round the corner. The resemblance was remarkable. Paul Mayo, however, had a rich Hampshire accent and a spluttering laugh that would, in turn, convulse me. He was eccentric, lovable, with a great sense of the ridiculous. He had an obsession with pretending to be in love with Miss Bevis, a middle-aged, plain and prim accountant who worked part-time at the Playhouse. He was much given to singing as he painted and would always contrive to include Miss Bevis's name in the song in place of the real words. 'Some enchanted evening, you will see Miss Bevis, you will see Miss Bevis, across a crowded room,' he would warble. 'On top of Miss Bevis, all covered in snow,' was his version of 'Old Smokey'.

To eke out my meagre three pounds a week, I also signed on as a stage-hand to do the overnight striking and setting of the next production, because dress-rehearsal took place on Sunday to allow more time for lighting and dressing the set. Remember, these productions were of a much higher standard than I had hitherto been involved in. This stage-hand's job went on all night but paid (I think) two pounds ten shillings for the one night, so nearly doubled my weekly wage. But hard, long work. We would still be at it, bleary-eyed and staggering slightly, when the actors came in at ten o'clock on the Sunday morning. How I wished I was one of them. Ivor Humphris, my friend of amateur days, was a stage-hand too, so we giggled most of the night away with Paul Mayo, but were never allowed to slack by Bob, the resident Stage Manager. The sets, I have to say, were always splendid in concept and detail and it was satisfying to be part of creating them, albeit during the early hours of the morning when all God-fearing men should be asleep.

For the first two or three productions I plodded round the town by day, and hung around the theatre in the evening, sometimes backstage, sometimes in the coffee bar above the foyer, living and breathing the heady atmosphere of the Playhouse. Nothing else mattered in my life except to be a part of it, however lowly. I felt I was contributing in some small way by my diligence in publicising our productions throughout the city and the varsity, the town and the gown. But I prayed that somehow, soon, Frank would give me a line or two on those hallowed and by now familiar boards. A butler, perhaps. A footman, perchance. Even a boots. A passer-by, either from left to right, or right to left, or even both ways. A member of the crowd. Surely to God a play with an enormous cast must turn up with a tiny, simple, impossible-to-mess-up part that Frank felt he could trust me with. Could he not see that I could cope with a couple of lines?

Frank Shelley did much more than that. He trusted me with a very sensitive and sympathetic character, beautifully written, in which I was to give a performance which, in my own opinion, was the best I ever achieved in four years at the Playhouse.

He came into the publicity office one morning clutching a script. 'Morning, gentlemen,' he bellowed, rattling the windows and Bert Lyon's false teeth. 'Would you mind, Bert? Want to speak to Ronnie alone.'

Bert bowed out, adjusting his dentures.

'Big cast next production; like you to look at the part of Peter Marti in this,' he said, flinging down the script. 'Give me a reading in about half an hour. I'll be in my office,' and he breezed out, leaving me gasping. The play was *Pick-up Girl*, which sounds terrible but was in fact a very good courtroom drama, set in America, about a teen-age girl who, because of rumour and prejudice, is falsely accused of being a prostitute. My character, a young violinist, speaks in her defence and also carries a twist in the plot that makes the part, although small, very important and a good show-piece.

I was so keen to impress Frank that I gave a reading charged with a sort of nervous energy which obviously impressed him. He agreed to let me play it then and there and I spent the rest of the week in a rainbow daze of delight. It goes without saying that by the time the first rehearsal came, I knew the part inside out.

The girl playing the leading character was Christine Pollon, married to the leading man Donald Hewlett.

They seemed more affluent than the rest of the company – Donald was the one with the car, albeit a little match-box on wheels. Christine was Welsh. She had that inner sparkle that I find nearly all Welsh girls have – such an irresistible quality, combined as it was with warmth and a great sense of fun. In any event, I was deeply attracted to Christine from the first rehearsal. Of course, being married to Donald she behaved very properly, but she soon knew that I was hopelessly in love with her. In the play, as we gazed at each other, she in the dock, I in the witness-box, her eyes conveyed so much of what seemed genuine love that I yearned for her. Although of course I realised when I came off-stage that she had merely been acting the part superbly. Off-stage she was always warm and friendly towards me and, although nothing physical ever manifested itself, we enjoyed each other's company.

I wasn't in the next play, but the one after was called *He Who Gets Slapped*, a circus play, and I was cast as one of the two supporting clowns called, I think, Tilly and Polly. What a joy to put on actual clown make-up, and to have the opportunity to use my new-found skill (now over a year old) – the backward roll. I put it in wherever I could, although I nearly kicked the leading lady's teeth out at rehearsals. I eventually managed the trick landing on a chair placed behind me, on which was a collapsible top hat. I squashed it flat. Big laugh. Of course, I didn't wear my glasses during a performance and one evening I marched on, saw the black blur on the chair, did my backward roll, and landed on the theatre cat, which was allowed to wander around in this particular production, giving atmosphere to the circus tent. The cat, winded at first, suddenly screeched and shot straight into the audience, severely scratching a large lady who tried to calm it down. It was decided that thereafter the cat would not be allowed on the stage, but no one could find it to tell it so. In fact I don't remember ever seeing it again.

After a few productions, I began to be regularly cast in each play, so, without any actual policy decision by Frank, I simply was not around to do any publicity to speak of, being always now tied up with rehearsals. This of course was bliss to me. For the first time in my theatrical career I was simply an actor, without any other backstage commitments or responsibilities.

A great weight was off my shoulders. I got cast in a variety of roles, straight as well as comedy, and loved them all. Frank Shelley himself would occasionally play a part that took his fancy and he announced one morning his intention to appear in *A Cuckoo in the Nest*, a very funny farce by the master, Ben Travers.

He had cast all the parts except one, an old woman. I was playing the pot-boy at the village inn, called, I think, Alfred.

'How can you be in it, Frank? You've cast it all,' I remember saying to him in the pub.

'Not quite, dear chap. I'm playing the landlady.'

And indeed he did. A wonderful costume and make-up, a dragon-woman. One of Frank's funniest performances. In one scene I had to help this old harridan onto the table to light the oil lamp. I loved to provoke Frank into an ad-lib whenever I could, and one night I put my hand up his skirt and pinched his upper leg. 'Ooh!' he screeched in his crabbed contralto. 'No one's been there since the Armistice!' You could tell he enjoyed that scene immensely every night.

Plays are bound to go somewhat out of sequence here, but it really doesn't matter. There were certainly lots of productions between *Pick-up Girl* and the Christmas show, and I remember Christine and me spending much innocent time together. I tended to follow her about like an obedient puppy, shopping round Oxford, always happy to be in her company, worshipping the ground she walked on, the counters she leaned on. The Christmas show, however, was the first time I saw her legs.

The pantomime was *Cinderella*, in a rather eccentric version written by Frank Shelley himself. It was the second time it had been performed at the Playhouse and I had seen the previous one when an amateur. Mike Ford and I had climbed onto the stage on the last night and presented the two ugly sisters with a bottle of brown ale each, God knows why. We must have appeared absolute idiots. I can only plead extreme youth. The two sisters took it very well – one was one of my favourite actors at the Playhouse, John Moffatt, whom I have mentioned earlier. The other was a very young, very slim Tony Hancock, before he became the national hero of later years.

So I was delighted now to be part of it. But I was even more delighted that Christine was Prince Charming, exhibiting yards of fish-netted leg. And she was charming indeed as the Prince. One can see why the tradition of girls playing boys has always been popular. They look so irresistibly attractive.

I played only two small roles: the Baron (always a boring part and in this production, no exception) and a mad Spanish character, new to the traditional story, called Don Moustachio Candelabra di Tapioca. I did a frenzied Spanish dance with one of the sisters, during which I sang extraordinary lyrics. It went very well, but I would still have preferred to have played the ugly sister, opposite Donald Hewlett.

The weeks went by and then a play came along which threw Christine and me much closer together. It was called *Point of Departure* by Jean Anouilh, a modern version of the Orpheus and Eurydice theme. Christine and I were cast as the two tragic lovers. Lying together in a big old-fashioned brass bed, wearing not very much, kissing her as lovers kiss, was almost too much for me to bear.

There came the inevitable time one afternoon in the dressing-room when I could resist no longer and did my best to persuade her to go further. She kissed me briefly, and said no. It just wouldn't do, it wouldn't be fair to Donald. She left and, alone in the room, I buried my head in my arms and burst into tears.

'What's the matter, old chap?'

It was Donald, Christine's husband. I looked up in surprise at his kindly, sympathetic face.

'I'm in love with your wife,' I blurted out.

'Well, never mind,' he said simply, 'a lot of men are. You'll get over it.' He touched me on the shoulder. 'You have a good cry. I'll see you later.'

I never saw Christine again after they left the Playhouse. Some years later they were divorced and Donald Hewlett has remained a friend to this day.

12

Jessie Matthews, the famous musical comedy film star, was booked to appear with the company in a play called *Larger Than Life* adapted from Somerset Maugham's novel, *Theatre*. She had always been a great favourite of mine ever since I had first seen her being enchanting in films like *Evergreen* and *Gangway*. I was fascinated by the way she could kick her leg so high that she banged herself on the ear. In fact I was for a time concerned that she might go deaf until I noticed that she only did it with one leg. Obviously to make sure that she retained full hearing in one of her ears, at least.

She duly arrived and was charming.

'Welcome to Oxford,' I said.

'Pardon?' she said, confirming as I thought my worst fears for her deafness. But she just hadn't heard me; there was nothing wrong with her hearing, because I later mentioned the high kicks and made her laugh. Naturally, she was now somewhat older.

'There are lots of places I can't get my leg nowadays, more's the pity,' she said. She was certainly a game girl, and I admired her a lot.

Which made what happened during that week even more unfortunate. I have to confess that there were, in my entire career, two occasions on which I appeared before the public having had too much to drink. This was the first time.

I had been cast in this backstage drama in the part of the Stage Manager – a part which lasted all of two minutes, and required no make-up, simply a warehouse coat. Rather like my earlier role at the Pavilion, Rhyl. Except that I didn't spend most of the play in my digs along the sea-front. On this occasion, the Jessie Matthews production, I spent most of it in the Gloucester Arms. I must explain that the pub in question was across the alleyway from the stage-door of the Playhouse and a previous electrician who liked a jar or two had arranged an electric buzzer to be fixed in the saloon bar, giving warning of the rise of the curtain for each act of the performance. This was a permanent fixture and was a great help to members of the audience who popped out during the interval, as well as the stage-staff. My two-minute role was five minutes after the curtain rose on Act Three.

Duncan, my erstwhile head of publicity, had only days ago introduced me to iced red wine and water, a drink which in the warm summer evening's atmosphere was rather more intoxicating than I realised. We sat engaged in pleasant conversation from 7.30 or so until about 9.15 when the buzzer went for the start of Act Three.

'Good heavens, doesn't the time fly,' I said, 'I must get in.' I got to my feet and realised I had overdone it. Trying to conceal the fact, I walked carefully out of the pub, across the alley and in the stage-door. Behind the door, on a hook, hung my warehouse coat. I put it on and went through the pass door onto the back of the stage. Thinking I would be better sitting down to await my entrance, I pulled a chair over near the door to the set, completely forgetting that Miss Matthews was shortly due out of that door for a quick change. While I was negotiating the chair, she flew out and ran slap-bang into me. She pitched forward and sort of rolled head over heels, her legs going places that they hadn't been for years, helped by the fact that her evening dress split from top to bottom or rather from hem to bottom, revealing underwear very similar to that which we all know and love from her early films.

I scrambled to help her up which wasn't easy, both of us tripping over her torn dress. Naturally, she was livid and had every right to be. She hardly spoke to me again during the run, although she did include me in the list of presents left in our dressing-rooms on the last night. But it was another four or five years before I touched a drink (for the last time ever) before a performance.

This brief performance as a Stage Manager in the play seemed fraught with danger, because a couple of nights after the collision, I had waited for my cue, keeping well out of the way of Jessie as she flew out of the door, and then entered. My part consisted of speaking on the telephone to a minion, ordering various items, props and so forth, to be brought at once to the set of the play-within-a-play. I entered, sat on the stool and dialled a number, and the stool collapsed beneath me, dumping me on my back. Some of the audience thought it part of the show, but most realised it was a mistake, as was obvious when I ad-libbed, 'Oh, and Charlie, send me up another stool while you're at it,' getting a round of applause. That sort of applause, an immediate response to what they know is a spontaneous funny remark, is always the best, the most exciting. It was only when I got off the stage that I realised Jessie Matthews was due to sit on that stool five minutes later. I felt I was somewhat vindicated in that I had prevented another embarrassing show of legs for our visiting star.

We had at this time a very amusing chap in the company by the name of Francis Matthews. He filled the role of Juvenile or Juvenile Lead and occasionally, Leading Man. He is, I think, of Lancashire origin, and of an irresistibly whimsical and jocular nature. A wonderful Clive Popkiss in *Rookery Nook* and a completely convincing leading man in the weepie, *Random Harvest.*

He stays mainly in my memory because of his immense charm off-stage as well as on. Kind and generous on-stage, and of a truly witty humour off. Later, on television, he displayed these qualities to advantage as Paul Temple, the famous sleuth.

It was he who related to me one of my favourite land-lady stories. The theatrical seaside landlady who gossips, over the wall, to her neighbour.

'That milkman,' she says, 'is so full of himself.'

'Cheeky sod,' says her neighbour. 'Do you know, Nancy,' she says, 'he boasts he's slept with every woman in the street except one.'

'Really?' says our landlady.

'Truth,' says her neighbour.

'By heck,' says our landlady, 'I bet it's that stuck-up bitch at number 29.'

This story, he swears, is true. I would like to believe him but in any case, what does it matter? A joke is a joke, and a good laugh is a treasure beyond rubies.

During the early part of my stay at Oxford, Frank Shelley, along with presumably the governors of the Playhouse, decided to start a school of drama. Much more well-intentioned than the travesty of the six girl students at Aylesbury. The students had proper acting lessons during the afternoons and were given small parts from time to time in the professional productions. Two or three boys and maybe eight or nine girls enrolled with the school and I naturally mixed with them, as all the company did, in the coffee bar and greenroom. One of the girls was to become one of the country's leading actresses, and a Dame of the British Empire – Maggie Smith. The story of how I once told her she would never make it as an actress and should give it up has been told so often I will not go into it again here.

The girl to whom I was steadily more attracted each day was another student named Jean Wagstaff. She was a pretty, sporting, healthy type of girl with a wide attractive smile and no affected side to her nature. She seemed to like me and was not otherwise attached to any other fellow. Christine Pollon was glad to see me interested in someone else, although our tenuous relationship was already much diminished.

Jean was lovely. I can't remember first kissing her, although it may have been as a result of the night we all went midnight-bathing in the river. I was only two or three years older than the students and I had to a large extent taken up with them as a group. Jean was about eighteen then. It was suggested one hot summer's night that after the performance of some play or other, in which two or three of the students had parts, we should go for a midnight swim. It was also suggested by one of the party, a big boisterous maid whom I shall call Brenda, that the event should take place in the nude. Brenda, I should add, was not even a student, but a sort of hanger-on, a camp follower and, it has to be said, rather more theatrical than the rest of the group. She was the sort of girl who stood out from the crowd, mainly due to her forty-two-inch bust. She had already made it clear that she longed to pursue a theatrical career, and I had warned her that with a figure as curvy as that, she could never be a straight actress. But as a nude swimmer, she would be sure to outstrip the others. The word breaststroke began to take on a new meaning. But enough of this punning.

Off we all went armed with towels, white wine and crisps, to a stretch of deserted river which was free of reeds and safe for a swim. Some of the girls kept on bits and pieces of clothing, but most of us were fairly uninhibited. It was warm, moonlit, idyllic weather and we splashed and sported in the cool water, with the inevitable chases and romps which are bound to ensue when a group of young people are without benefit of modest clothing. Brenda left nothing on, or indeed anything to the imagination, as she pranced and sprawled on the grass. Her bosom was wonderful, and her hips enough to drive a man mad. I couldn't help but make a beeline for her as she cavorted. Dodging the stinging-nettles we fell to the ground and a bout of kissing and cuddling, all too brief, followed. Brenda was soon telling me she was a virgin, and didn't do that sort of thing.

'But I like to tease,' she said.

'You're very good at it,' I said, 'you could get a name for it.' I didn't tell her what name, but by what she had said, she half-knew anyway.

We were soon all drying ourselves and, more fun, each other, quaffing warm white wine to wash down the ready-salted crisps. Jean, who had kept on her pants, I remember, sat with one of the boys who would not have been by nature interested in her physically. I went over and joined them, and he took the opportunity to slide away.

'I thought you were with Brenda,' she said, with her pretty mouth full of crisps. I think it must have been then that I kissed her. I know that she pretended to have nothing to do with me for a while, but we did walk home arm in arm, and from then on considered each other to be close, as they say. In the matter of a few weeks, we became even closer, as close as a boy and girl can get without actually living together. The relationship developed, and Jean and I were together until I left Oxford. I would spend Sundays with her and her parents at their house at the far end of the Woodstock road, almost in Wolvercote. Just down the lane was the famous Trout Inn at Godstow, which featured in the American film version of *Charley's Aunt* and was one of our favourite haunts. I noticed a year or so ago that it was much favoured by Inspector Morse too, which shows his inherent good taste. It is right on the river.

The river in Oxford, called variously the Thames, the Isis, or the Cherwell, is a great contributor to the beauty of the city, and featured largely in my enjoyment of life when I was young. There is still nothing so peaceful, nothing so delightful as drifting in a punt along a shaded backwater, with only a lazy paddle to steer you along past reedy banks, through sunlit meadows. It was a constant pastime for lads and lasses, be they varsity students or locals. Some were energetic enough to use the punt-pole, and go hurtling by with great determination, a gleam in their eye and sweat on their brow. I often wondered where they were trying to get to, bearing in mind they had to come back the same way to return their punt from whence they hired it. Much too much like hard work, I would think, as the wash from their wake lapped at the polished mahogany sides of our drifting boat, occasionally splashing the velvet cushions on which Jean and I reclined, she trailing her fingers and sometimes her toes in the water.

This is my golden memory of Oxford, and always will be. My best time. If I were to have to pick the absolute quintessence of this time, it would be May morning. On the first day of May, at six o'clock in the morning, the choir of Magdalen College gather on top of Magdalen Tower, which is on the banks of the river, and sing madrigals to welcome summer. The traffic, such as there was in those days, would stop or be stopped by the police, and the whole area would be hushed, silent. The clocks struck six and, high above us on the tower, the crystal voices would be heard, floating down to us on the still morning air. The people on the ground listened, breathless, to the crisp beauty of the church harmonies for perhaps fifteen or twenty minutes, and then silence; it was over. The place to listen was, of course, from a punt on the river. The water reflected the sound, so beautiful that it usually brought a tear or two to the eye.

After it was over, the breakfast-party would commence. We moved off downstream, and the girls in the group sorted out utensils and provisions. We moored the boat, set up an oil-stove in the meadow and cooked bacon, sausages and fried bread. Nothing ever before or since tasted as good as that May morning breakfast.

We were doing some great plays at the Playhouse. *The Lady's Not for Burning* by Christopher Fry was a splendid piece of theatre. I had seen it in London, and when I was cast in the five-minute role of a drunken tramp who thinks he has died and gone to Heaven, I tried in vain to remember the part. I happened to have a programme of the London production (John Gielgud, impeccable). Looking through it, I discovered that the part had been played by Esme Percy and remembered that I hadn't been able to hear a word he said. When I got the script, however, I found the dialogue to be marvellously funny.

Christopher Fry himself came to see our production at the dress-rehearsal. I had decided to play it Irish, as it was full of religious misquotes, like 'peace on earth and good tall women'. I was expecting him to comment on this unscripted use of accent but to my delight, he said, 'You know, when you read it again it's written Irish, isn't it?'

The local critics, both city and varsity, gave me glowing notices. The university magazines had amongst their critics many names who were to have a distinguished career in show business.

Kenneth Tynan had just left university when I started at the Playhouse, but I particularly remember Brian Tesler, now a TV mogul; Patrick Dromgoole, afterwards a respected television director and Ned Sherrin, 'a man,' to use his own words about me, 'who needs no introduction from me, and so shall get none'. Michael Codron, the theatrical impresario, was also up at Oxford at the time and could often be seen with the aforementioned notables in the coffee bar at the Playhouse. This little room was to a great extent the theatrical hub of the student body. It was, of course, strictly teetotal during the day but in the evening, during performances, served as the bar and featured as a backdrop to an episode in my relationship with Jean. An evening which, even now, fills me with shame.

I was and still am very stage-struck when it comes to meeting the stars of my profession. I was recently quite dry-mouthed and completely overcome with nerves when I met Alan Alda, my hero from *MASH*, who was as charming off-screen as on. And in my Oxford days, I thrilled to see in the street West End stars who were appearing at the New Theatre round the corner. This was the big number one touring theatre which took all the pre-London shows.

One of my favourite British film actors was at that time William Hartnell, years before *Doctor Who*, when he played tough navy or army NCOs, or mean crooks and the like. I was sitting in the coffee bar one evening when he walked in. He was not at the New Theatre, so I was not ready for him at all. I leapt to my feet to introduce myself in a very forward fashion, and found him very friendly. He offered me a drink; we sat at the bar on the high stools and talked. I bought him a drink; he bought me another. He was in Oxford to see the Director of the play at the New Theatre and having done that, his time was his own. I bought another round of gin and tonics. Gin was not at that time my drink; I was a beer and/or wine merchant. Consequently, by the time we finally parted he had had enough and I had had too much. Suddenly, he wasn't there and I sat for a while, rather bemused, before finally deciding I should make a move. It was then, and only then, that I remembered I was supposed to be going to Jean's house to have dinner with her parents.

Overwhelmed with embarrassment and regret, I tottered out and caught the bus to Wolvercote. I was now an hour late and sat there in the front seat in a haze of gin for what seemed like an eternity. Eventually I staggered off the bus and crossed the large area of grass which served as a roundabout. Every time I pass it now on my way to London, forty years later, the picture is as clear as if it were yesterday. To be truthful it is much clearer, for on that evening it was an alcoholic blur through which suddenly appeared my girl, Jean. She at once summed up the situation, and I received a slap on the face so hard that it not only felled me to the ground, but in the process knocked a lens out of my glasses and sent it flying. I was now blind in one eye and blind drunk in both eyes.

Still furious, she hunted about for ages among the grass, but we never found the lens. The rest of the evening is now a complete blank, but I know it took a week or two for my Jean to bring herself to even speak to me. I was full of remorse and never stopped apologising to her parents when I was at last allowed to meet them again. Jean's old grandfather – who was as they say 'a character', meaning that he occasionally said embarrassing things in front of company – didn't help by saying, 'When I was a lad *I* never went home half-drunk. Unless I ran out of money.'

He had some very funny patter, well-rehearsed no doubt, but always apt. At high tea on a Sunday, he would help himself to pickled onions and remark, 'The secret of good health is to eat onions. That is, if you can keep it a secret.' Or 'Now, Jean my girl, watch those cream cakes. She who indulges, bulges.' Jean, fortunately, never had any trouble with her figure, but I was constantly keeping an eye on it.

I have a feeling that I was beginning to fill out, although when I played Hercule Poirot in the first of three plays we did in which he appeared, the local press critic commented that, 'Ronald Barker is even more dapper and perky than ever . . . and acts with splendid flourish. He is, if anything, a shade too dapper, for his smart Palm Beach suit shows up his wiry young man's figure, which ill matches the receding hair on his dome-like head.' (A wig which took over an hour to fit and painstaking make-up so as not to show the join.) I loved playing the Belgian detective, and the play was so popular that within a few weeks we did the second and the third in the Poirot trilogy. Hastings, the faithful assistant, was always played by Donald Hewlett and we had a very rewarding and enjoyable time playing together, as indeed we always seemed to. Donald was marvellous in the Ben Travers farces, and we would have a hard time keeping straight faces when on-stage together.

The Poirot plays with their long cast lists required that extra actors be brought in for 'special weeks' as they were known, even though plays at Oxford actually lasted a fortnight. Two actresses in particular gave me a few frights during the course of my scenes with them. Poirot is on-stage all the time in these dramas, so if anything goes wrong, he is bound to be involved. One actress failed to bring on two vital letters which Poirot has to read aloud. She opened her handbag, and it was empty. She actually showed me, and the audience, the empty bag.

'Did you perhaps drop them in the hall?' I enquired, which was the best I could do under the circumstances, but which could have been better worded, conjuring up the picture of this girl dropping her knickers in front of the butler.

'I may have done,' she ad-libbed back, increasing the titter from the audience into a fair-sized laugh.

'I will see if I can find them,' I announced, and darted outside amid scattered applause. I grabbed the letters from the prop table and went back on-stage.

I tried to play down the incident, but of course the audience wouldn't leave it alone. Every time I referred to the letters, they were thinking knickers, and the poor girl was glad to finish the scene and get off. But by then I had decided to wrap up the incident once and for all in the minds of the audience. As she rose to leave, I added to my farewell, 'And try not to be so careless in the future, madame. Losing things like that can get you into trouble.' A round of applause from the audience and the joke was over.

More worrying than that was a lady of some age who played a suspect and never knew a line of the script during rehearsals. Came the first night, and nothing altered. I asked a question and instead of giving me a long explanation, she merely shrugged with a look of panic in her eyes. I knew that she was hopelessly lost. I had learnt my part but naturally enough not hers.

'Listen!' I suddenly said in desperation, 'there is someone creeping about outside,' and I hurried out through the French windows to find there was indeed someone creeping about. It was the prompter, with the prompt-book. I grabbed it, stared at the next couple of speeches and came back through the windows. 'I could see nothing,' I said. 'Perhaps, madame, you were going to tell me about the telephone call you received last night?' This cue reminded her of her line and off we went once more. Two minutes later, she forgot everything again.

Three times I pretended to hear something, rushed off, read the script and rushed on again. The poor woman was by now a quivering jelly. My jelly wasn't too steady either, I may say. 'Madame,' I finally ad-libbed, 'go to the library and write down everything you know. I will study it later.' She made a shaky but thoroughly relieved exit. Poirot, in spite of everything, remained one of my favourite characters.

There were many others, in many other plays. Good plays. Good stuff. *Journey's End* by R C Sherriff was memorable for me. It is a drama about the British Army in the First World War, and takes place entirely in a dug-out in the front line in France. It is a thoroughly atmospheric piece, and the set was so realistic – dust and mud and timber, with Mike Ford producing truly authentic sound effects of the continual bombardment of the British lines.

I played Sergeant Trotter, a ranker who was the main comedy element in the play. He was a man who was constantly hungry, and during the course of each performance I was required to eat four full meals. Usually one can fake eating to a large extent, but much was made of the fact that Trotter ate everything in sight, both his own and other people's share, so I really had to consume soup, bully beef, a breakfast of bacon and fried bread, then a tea of doorsteps of bread and plum jam, and finally another bacon breakfast. All consumed with absolute relish. Needless to say, on the Saturday evening, having just done the play in the afternoon, I was coming off-stage and throwing up, only to have to return to another large plateful in the very next scene.

Aside from the eating, however, the part had a wonderful sympathetic quality. When he finally lays down his knife and fork for the last time and leaves the dugout to meet his Maker (courtesy of a sniper's bullet), the play's message – of war's unfairness towards ordinary men, caught up in it whether they will or no – comes across like a tidal wave. At the end of the play when all its occupants have been killed, the dugout receives a direct hit. It collapses in clouds of dust onto the body of a young soldier and the curtain falls. When it rises again, the eerie greenish light from a flare illuminates the dugout; the dust still falling and all the dead men – or their ghosts – standing to attention as the last post is played on a solo bugle. This moment is I think the most moving of any I have been involved in on the stage. There was absolute silence as the curtain rose and fell on this, the only curtain-call. Only when it had settled, and the house-lights went on in the auditorium, did the audience burst into rapturous applause. Sometimes there were cheers. Good plays. Good stuff.

13

Charley's Aunt is a good play. *Charley's Aunt* is good stuff. We did it as the Christmas show one year, with Donald Hewlett as the Aunt. It was, I suppose, the most commercially successful thing the Playhouse did while I was there, and it ran for seven weeks to full houses. The play has been in existence for over a hundred years and is still funny, still popular. I played Brassett, the college servant, but not as the usual long-suffering manservant. He is in fact a college 'scout', and here we were right in the middle of the territory, right where the play is set, in an Oxford college. So of course I played him as an irascible local man with a broad Oxfordshire accent, a man that the audience knew like the backs of their collective hands, the man who served them in the butcher's or the greengrocer's every day. There was thus an immediate rapport as soon as I opened my mouth. For the audience, this was a new voice from me, and they loved him. He has forty-two entrances during the three acts, more than any other character I've ever played, and I thoroughly enjoyed every one of them. I later used the voice for Able Seaman Fatso Johnson in *The Navy Lark*.

The Oxfordshire accent (not to be confused with an Oxford accent) is a lovely, gravelly, comic sound which lends itself to all those yokel jokes about the country boy's visit to the big city. Like the yokel who goes on a day trip to Southend and gets drunk. A policeman stops him on the promenade and says, 'Here, you're drunk and disorderly. I could put you in prison for a month for that.'

'Oh, no you can't,' says the yokel, 'Oi be only 'ere for the day.'

Frank Shelley enjoyed himself enormously during rehearsals, and was besotted with the whole piece, watching every night's performance and coming round afterwards with notes, extra gags and so forth. He decided after the play had been running a fortnight that a special effort should be made on the publicity front, to see for how long we could fill the theatre. He decreed that he, Donald, the two girls in the show and myself should make morning tours round the local Oxford villages dressed in costume, to attract extra press coverage and distribute leaflets. Poor Donald had to dress as the Aunt, while Frank and I merely wore college blazers, mortar-boards and gowns.

This was fine, albeit tiring, but Frank decided that we should all carry a little something to keep out the cold of the January weather. He was not talking portable electric fires, either. He was talking whisky. He issued us each with a hip-flask and like a child going for a picnic, he started his when we'd been on the road for only ten minutes. Frank was driving one car, Donald the other, and as I was travelling with Frank, I was rather concerned but could do nothing except grit my teeth and hope. The hope was fortified with a swig or two from my own flask. At each stop, we would greet the villagers, distribute our leaflets and inevitably end up in the pub. Donald, very sensibly, kept off the hard stuff, as he had a very heavy show to do that evening, but Frank would thoroughly enjoy himself, quipping with the locals and buying drinks all round.

I loved listening to all the droll country characters with their native wit. I said to one weather-beaten character that I presumed he was in some way connected with agriculture. 'No, farming,' he said.

'Isn't that the same thing?' said I.

'Well,' he replied, 'it's similar, only with farming you really do it.'

Frank, in his element – fortified and, in some cases, fiftified, by his hip-flask – was highly entertaining. At a pub on the outskirts of Witney where we had visited the girls in the blanket factory, Frank and I got into conversation with a large craggy-faced son of toil at the bar, while Donald and the girls were entertained at a nearby table.

'I've got a conundrum to ask you,' he said, addressing Frank.

'I'm surprised you can even say it,' was the reply. 'Carry on.'

The ton of soil, ignoring the jibe, continued, 'I'm thinking of a person. My father is their father. My mother is their mother. But they are not my sister, and nor are they my brother.'

'That rhymes,' boomed Frank, rattling the bar glasses and the barmaid's earrings.

'Yes, but who is it?' said the man.

'No idea.'

'It's me!'

'You?' said Frank.

'Me,' said the man.

'Incredible,' said Frank, obviously impressed. He immediately went over to Donald at the table. I followed.

'I'm thinking of a person, Donald,' said Frank. He

didn't attempt the rhyme. 'Same father and mother as me, but not my sister or brother. Who is it?'

Donald didn't know. 'Who is it, Frank?' Frank beamed. 'Well, you'll never believe it, but it's that fat man over at the bar.'

They were fun-filled days, but I needed a bit of a lie-down in the afternoons before the forty-two entrances every night. Frank so loved the production that he revived it a few months later, with himself playing the Aunt. He was quite different from Donald Hewlett in the role, less boyish and dashing but much more eccentric. He was also in the habit of taking a few liberties with the text, one night asking the girls in the drawing-room scene, seated at the piano, whether they would prefer him to play 'Mozart, or "The Blue Balls of Scotland".'

My social life was now almost entirely concerned with Jean, with whom I would spend most Sundays: lunch at her parents' house, long afternoon wanders in the countryside looking for lonely spots to plight our troth, and returning, our troths more often than not well and truly plighted, to high tea, ham and cucumber sandwiches and a bit of ribbing from Jean's father and grandfather.

They owned a gentleman's outfitters in the area known as St Ebbes, a wonderful old warren of narrow streets and little period houses and shops. Nowadays in the nineties, it would be a pedestrian precinct, full of little antique shops, pottery and craft boutiques but then, in the fifties, you could find so many wonderful old establishments: ironmongers, barbers, painters and decorators' merchants. But between the fifties and the nineties came, unfortunately, the sixties when some insane architects and town planners, with the full blessing of an equally philistine council, decided to bash it all to the ground and build the Westgate Shopping Centre. But who am I to be grumbling and regretting and agonising over this disastrous decision? Merely a member of that large and powerless group known as the public.

There, I've had my little gripe. Back to the fifties when Messrs Wagstaff, senior and junior, ran their little men's shop. Jean's father, who could see that Jean and I were what is known as 'serious', ventured to suggest that the acting profession was not a sufficiently solid foundation on which to base a secure and happy marriage.

'Why not come and work with us at the shop?' he suggested. 'One day it would be yours. Forget all this floating [the word may have been 'poncing'] about on the stage. I mean to say, you are very good and all that, but I can't see you getting very far after you leave here. It's a bit of a dead-end job, isn't it?'

Fortunately, when we were alone, Jean told me to take no notice of his remarks. 'You stay where you are, my darling, you're going to get somewhere. I wouldn't want to marry back into the family.' Which I thought was a rather good way of putting it. She had heard enough about the family business ever since she'd been a small girl. Now she wanted something different, and so most certainly did I. No more was said about it, and I continued to practise my craft, almost always excited by the prospect of the next production, greedy to take on another character, another performance, another make-up.

Night Must Fall, the wonderfully atmospheric and creepy play by Emlyn Williams, was another chance for Frank to dabble in publicity. He thought it would make a wonderful story for the press if he announced that the principal part of Danny – the young bellhop and murderer who carried the head of his last victim in a hatbox – was such a difficult part to cast that he could not make up his mind between me and John Randall, another actor in the company. John was quite different from me: thin, gaunt, capable of being very sinister. He was also, by the by, an innate prankster (but not in this play!).

Frank announced that John would play the part the first week and I would attempt it the second week. This was fine for the press and the public, some of them coming twice to compare the two of us. But the cast complained bitterly, having to come in for another dress-rehearsal with me, the new Danny, on the second Sunday, traditionally the 'weekend away', many of them having flats in London. However they put up with it and I thoroughly enjoyed the chance to play the lead, a part I had coveted ever since my amateur days when I had played a smaller role in the same play. The critics were very nice, and mentioned my 'powerful charm'. It must have been this which triggered off a bizarre and exhausting interlude at the hands of a girl some two or three years my senior who suddenly appeared on the social scene.

On the second night of the play, as I was removing my make-up, there came a knock at the door. 'Come in, I'm decent,' I called. In walked a complete stranger, a girl whom for the sake of propriety I will call Freda.

'Hello, my name's Freda, I'm understudying at the New Theatre, and I've just seen your show, and I think you're fantastic.'

With that, she flung her arms round me and kissed me in a way that needed responding to. Her hands were everywhere, and she and I stood locked in an embrace that knocked the wind out of me.

'Hang on,' I managed to gasp, 'who are you? I don't even know you.'

'What has that got to do with anything?' she breathed, and went into the tackle again. This time we sort of collapsed onto the rather grubby carpet of the dressing-room.

As I came up for air, she murmured, 'Do you like the look of me?'

'You're very lovely,' I replied.

'Lock the door,' she commanded. I locked the door, and was dragged to the floor. Clothes were torn, buttons flew in all directions.

Three-quarters of an hour later we emerged from the dressing-room, she bright-eyed, me exhausted, having experienced everything the lady had to offer. God, I thought, I've only known her an hour. We haven't been introduced.

We went to a different pub, not the Gloucester Arms where all the others would be and where news of my escort might have got back to Jean.

She drank beer.

'I do usually,' I said, 'but tonight I need a stiff one.'

'Anything you say.' She told me she was on tour, understudying the leading lady at the New Theatre for that week only. After a couple of drinks, she decided we should go for a walk. I protested that I was tired, that I had to rehearse in the morning, but she would hear none of it. 'Nonsense,' she said, grabbing my arm and marching me out of the pub. She was a very determined and forceful young woman, and so sensually attractive that I went, like a lamb to the slaughter. 'Where?' she demanded.

'Where what?' I played for time.

'You know what,' she said.

I led her to the quiet spot on the banks of the river, the place where we had bathed at midnight. To the very spot where Brenda had told me she was a virgin.

'Your usual haunt, Ronnie? The scene of previous successes?'

'No, the scene of a previous failure. She was a virgin.'

'Weren't we all, darling? Now, let's get this straight –' and she moved into the attack.

I staggered into my house at five o'clock in the morning. I was a wreck, one of the walking wounded, or rather, one of the bicycling wounded, having had to ride back from the city. I collapsed into bed, saddle-sore, and fell into a deep sleep for all of three hours. My alarm clock woke me in time to climb back on my bike and head for rehearsals at ten o'clock. What a woman, I thought. I wonder if I shall ever see her again?

I did, the next night. There she was again, fresh as a daisy, smart as new paint, ready for a repeat performance or two.

'Come on, I liked it by the river. Let's go. The weather's beautiful.' I couldn't resist her, she was so indescribably sexy, but I did insist that as I had just strangled an old lady on-stage, I must be allowed a Scotch or two before taking on another opponent at wrestling.

I managed to get home by 2.30 a.m. this time, as she said she must get some beauty sleep. 'My boyfriend's coming down to see me tomorrow, so I can't see you.'

I breathed an inward sigh of relief. 'So you've got a regular boyfriend then?'

'Of course. I can't rely on finding someone like you every town we go to. You're an exception.' She smiled, putting a stranglehold on me. 'But if the boyfriend's coming down, you're out. He exhausts me.' Christ, I thought, he must be King Kong.

So on Thursday I was able to phone Jean and ask her to come down after the show. I was terrified that this insatiable girl would spoil my relationship with Jean and thought that if I took Jean for a drink on Thursday, I would be safe from Freda's clutches. Jean would then not come again the following day, Friday. We had a pleasant drink and a goodnight kiss at the bus-stop, and I retired to an early bed with great emotional and physical relief.

On Friday, there she was again. Freda the fantastic. This time, in spite of her radiant sexuality, I felt I must find some sort of excuse to get me off the hook.

'Groin strain,' I pleaded.

'Oh? How did that come about?' she demanded.

'You should know.'

'I don't believe you,' she replied and grabbed me right where the strain should have been. I let out a yell which I hoped was the consummation of all my acquired acting skills and this seemed to convince her. We had a drink in the pub as before away from the others, but as we said goodnight she put me to the test again with a well-directed left hand. I managed another groan of agony, and we said goodnight.

'But I'll be there tomorrow,' she announced. 'You'd better rest it. Try hot and cold bandages.'

Tomorrow was Saturday. Now the fat *was* in the fire. Jean always came to see the show on Saturday. All day I was in a muck sweat. I could think of no solution, apart from throwing myself under a number 3 bus. The hours ticked by and I arrived at the theatre still without any sort of answer to the problem.

A note awaited me at the stage-door.

Dearest thing. Cannot see you until later. I am having to play the part. The actress I am understudying has injured herself. See you about eleven. Hope you are fully recovered. You'll need to be. Love and things. Freda.

My reprieve had arrived. The great prison governor in the sky had come through trumps in the nick of time, in the shadow of the noose. I sent a note by way of reply

Dancing in the Moonlight

round to the New Theatre. *Good luck, sweetheart, tonight – and always.*

Our show finished just before 10.30 and by the time she arrived, Jean and I had gone.

Jean said, 'You were great in the play. You soon got changed and we're nice and early. Fancy going down by the river?'

I suppressed a hysterical sob. 'Not tonight, darling. I'm exhausted. I've been giving very tiring performances all week.'

14

The New Theatre where my recent assailant had taken over due to her 'principal's' illness, brought most excellent and marvellous shows to Oxford. I have already admitted what a fan I have always been where showbiz luminaries are concerned.

My first foray into the process of gratifying this craving to meet my heroes and heroines of stage and screen involved that great, sweet, charming and vulnerable British star, darling of so many married men, Celia Johnson. When I was but a lad, she came to do a play at the New called *Call Home the Heart*. It was on 5th November that I waited at the stage-door to get her autograph. No one else waited; I was the sole fan that evening. She was more charming than I could have expected. As she signed my programme, there was a large and alarming explosion from some fire-crackers on Gloucester Green. She jumped like a startled fawn, her eyes huge with fright.

'Heavens!' she exclaimed, which was probably as near swearing as she ever got.

'Don't worry, Miss Johnson,' I said protectively, 'it's only fireworks.'

'Heavens,' she again blasphemed, but her eyes, big and doe-like, calmed down. 'I'd forgotten it was Guy Fawkes.'

She smiled. 'I must get home, I've got cats.' A few moments out of her life, but I loved her for ever.

Jimmy Edwards' robust and fruity performances on stage and television had always been a great joy to me, so when I discovered that not only was he due to appear at the New Theatre, but also that he was a lifelong friend and fellow undergraduate of Donald Hewlett, our leading man, I was intrigued.

'We'll have a bit of a party after the show one night,' said Donald, 'and you can all meet him.'

At Donald and Christine's flat in Park Town, north Oxford, Jimmy Edwards sat there in the flesh, regaling us with stories while Donald recorded the events on his new wire recorder. (Yes, not tape, wire!) Somewhere I have a copy made on tape of that evening's jollities including precious moments when I managed to say something witty or silly enough to make the great man laugh. I was so proud of this tape, I remember. Little did I know that in years to come, my first real break in television was to be when I played feature parts with June Whitfield in Jimmy's own series. From that came *The Frost Report*, when I worked for the first time with Ronnie Corbett.

A play called *Golden Boy* by Clifford Odets brought Donald Houston back to the Playhouse. He was a hot property then, having been chosen to star in the film *The Blue Lagoon*. He was returning to the Playhouse where he had once been the Juvenile Lead and where as such I had seen him give many sensitive performances when I was just an amateur in the back row of the stalls. Now I was to act with him in a very tasty role as his Italian-Jewish brother-in-law. Jack Cassidy, our wardrobe master, was an old friend of Donald Houston, and Donald was staying with Jack. The high spot of the fortnight was a night spent carousing with them both, finishing up with me sleeping on Jack's floor and being woken up in the morning by Donald Houston asking me how I liked my eggs.

That breakfast to me was euphoric, cooked for me by a real star. Little ordinary me! Nowadays, when people say that meeting me has made their day, or the most wonderful thing that has ever happened to them or whatever, I still find it very difficult to believe and have to remind myself of those days when I felt exactly the same about those men and women I had worshipped from afar. I'm glad I can still remember. It makes me try to be as nice to fans as I would want my idols to be to me.

There is such a thing as overkill, of course, and I think Freda, the understudy with the mostest or at least the mostest oftenest, certainly overdid it during the week of *Night Must Fall*.

From that leading (and exhausting) role to a tiny part which I enjoyed thoroughly. *The Housemaster*, a school play by Ian Hay, has several schoolboys and girls in it, and Maggie Smith first made her mark as one of them. I played a character aged fourteen called Old Crump. My first appearance was when I knocked at the door of the Housemaster's study. I was a little doleful character in spectacles and school uniform, and I really felt fourteen. I knocked. 'Come in,' said the Master. I went in. The audience roared with laughter at my appearance. 'Get out,' said the Master. I left, having said nothing, to a round of applause. Time on stage, six or seven seconds. My most quickly earned exit round in the whole of my career.

It has to be borne in mind, of course, that this was a Monday night, the first night of the show, and in the audience were lots of members of the Playhouse Guild. This was a group of supporters who came to every production, half-price on Mondays, and who therefore knew all the actors and were very appreciative, to say the least. The Guild contained a few eccentrics as well but then Oxford has always had more than its fair share of eccentrics. One of its most famous sons, Lewis Carroll, was certainly so, and of course the Reverend Doctor Spooner's brain had a little kink in it which made him swap the first letters of words around. He incidentally also revived the practice of using the slang term, 'Bub', meaning brother, within the varsity.

He once gated a student for the rest of the term, saying to him, 'You have hissed all my mystery lectures, in fact you have tasted a whole worm. You will leave Oxford by the town drain tomorrow.' And as the unfortunate left the room, Dr Spooner said quietly and firmly to the rest of the students, 'And good riddance to bub radish.' The student eventually became quite high up in the Civil Service, but remained Bub Radish until his dying day.

As then, so in my day, no shortage of eccentrics. An ex-judge, a friend of Raymond Somerville the theatre manager, was more theatrical than many actors I've known. He would delight in telling us of the laughs he played for, and got, whilst sitting on the bench.

'I used to pretend to be a bit hard of hearing – it was expected of me,' he once said in the bar of the Randolph Hotel, where one could usually find him holding forth of an evening.

'I once said to a defendant, "Well, my man, have you anything to say before I pass sentence?" The man replied, "Bugger all, my Lord." "What did he say?" I asked the clerk of court, pretending not to have heard. "He said, 'Bugger all, my Lord'," to which I replied, "That's funny, I could have sworn I saw his lips move."'

I once asked him if he ever did any after-dinner speaking.

'No,' he said, 'but my wife is an after-dinner speaker. Also before and during.' A very entertaining eccentric.

Others were not quite so amusing; some there were who were downright boring, and needed dodging in the coffee bar of a morning. A tiny, absolutely spherical lady, who had so many chins that it looked as though she was looking at you over a pile of crumpets, would ask the most boring questions in a squeaky voice like chalk on a blackboard.

'How do you approach a part? How do you manage to be so different? Is it the make-up?'

These sort of questions are for most actors nearly always unanswerable, especially when you would rather be talking to some of the varsity girls who regularly frequented the place.

One large middle-aged lady, some fifty-five or sixty years old, took a fancy to me and was a constant nuisance. Frank had introduced me to her, saying she was a marvellous woman and a great supporter of the Playhouse. Afterwards he begged me to be nice to her, as he was hoping for some sort of massive donation to the theatre's funds at some point in the future. She was certainly mad about the place, coming two or even three times to a production, and was more often than not to be found in the coffee bar. She was in possession of a shrivelled little man of a husband: a drunk and a bore. She would hardly ever be seen with him and was constantly running him down in his absence. The lady was obviously looking for alternative male company. In fact, Frank seemed to be the man she was after.

Fairly thick-skinned, she missed most of Frank's innuendo; when they held a conversation, I was always reminded of Groucho Marx and Margaret Dumont. She was not unlike Margaret Dumont to look at, very ample and tall with that sort of bolster-like bosom. When she turned round you saw that she carried another one at the back as a spare, but king-size. Frank made fun of her unmercifully, which she took in good part, if and when she occasionally got the joke, calling him a 'naughty man' and giving him a playful slap. They both enjoyed being rude about her husband, and she would be constantly winking at me in between insults. She had quite a neat turn of phrase too. 'My husband is like a blotter. Soaks everything up in sight and gets everything back to front. I tell him something, it goes in one ear and straight out the other.'

Said Frank, 'That's because there's very little to stop it.' She groaned her agreement.

'I'm afraid he's going to hit me sometimes when he's plastered. Do you think it possible he could hit me, Frank?'

'He'd have a job missing you, Muriel. Great strapping woman like you, you must stand up to him.'

'Better still, sit on him.' I ventured a wisecrack of my own. 'That should knock the wind out of his sails.'

Frank laughed, but she turned to me. 'I need someone like you to protect me, Ronald dear,' she said, taking my hand in her oversized pair. Here we go, I thought. This time it was Frank's turn to wink at me.

'I'd love you to come up to the house, see my garden. I've a huge conservatory at the back.'

'We've noticed,' quipped Frank.

'Take no notice of this wicked man, Ronald, my peaches are at their best at the moment.'

I panicked a bit. 'You know very well I'm sort of engaged, Muriel,' I said hastily.

'I don't mean anything like that,' she gushed. 'I tell fortunes, and I'm a trained masseuse.'

'Oh my God,' said Frank, 'that does it. When shall I come?'

'I'm not talking to you, I'm talking to Ronald.'

I promised to think about it and got away as soon as I could, leaving Frank to cope.

The next thing we heard was that Muriel was giving a party for us at her big house in Iffley Road.

'Count me out,' I said to Frank. 'If she got me alone in an upper room, she'd be on me like a ton of bricks.'

'Ton and a half,' said Frank. 'But seriously, you must go, otherwise the Playhouse might lose her.' He was very insistent and he was the boss, after all.

The night arrived and we all turned up, the whole company. I desperately wanted Jean to go with me, and asked Muriel if I could bring a friend.

'Most certainly not,' she replied immediately. 'It's strictly the Playhouse company only.' So there I was on my own.

All went well for most of the party. I kept dodging Muriel and sticking with the crowd. There came a time when I had to go to the loo. I couldn't see Muriel anywhere, so it was with some trepidation that I popped upstairs, following temporary signs, and found a bathroom. I duly washed my hands before leaving and turned to the towel rail. A notice was pinned to the towel which said, *If you lay a finger on any of these towels, I will personally murder you in cold blood.* Terrified, I dried my hands on the curtains.

I had been there for some four hours and thought that I could now safely make my excuses and leave. I approached Muriel and said I really must be going.

'I have seen nothing of you all night,' she said reproachfully. 'Anyway, before you go, come up to my bedroom. There's something I must show you.'

She took my hand and dragged me upstairs.

'Where's your husband?' I said.

'Drunk and passed out in one of the guest-rooms,' she replied.

We reached her bedroom. She made a pretence of showing me a large nude painting on her wall. 'Me, when I was young,' with a wave of her hand. 'Now, admit it, you've been dodging me all evening. You're a naughty boy. You deserve to be taught a lesson.'

Good God, I thought, she's going to start knocking me about. Apologising profusely, I fled downstairs. She followed me to the front door. As I was within an inch of safety, I couldn't resist asking: 'Why was that notice on the towels?' She stared, then let out a howl.

'Oh, God in Heaven, that was for my husband. I should have taken that off before the guests arrived. How has everyone been managing?'

'Like me, I suppose – used the curtains.'

She let out another groan. 'Why ever didn't you tell me? You wicked boy. Come back here!'

But I was down the path and through the gate without waiting to see what sort of vengeance she would wreak upon me. The whole thing was so embarrassing to her that it was weeks before we saw her again, and by then she had a young varsity rugger type in tow. But I think I had a narrow escape from a fate worse than death. It might have, come to think of it, been actual death. By suffocation.

It may now be obvious that Frank Shelley and I had become much more pally with each other than in those first early days when I arrived in 1951. It was now 1954 and we had been concerned with some seventy or eighty plays together; he totally, and I to a greater or lesser extent, depending on the part.

Which was why when Frank announced that we were to do *The Love of Four Colonels*, Ustinov's very funny and satirical play, I was able to say to Frank, 'I think I'm right for the lead in that, Frank.'

It is a marvellous part, a really showy part. He is the wicked fairy and has to appear as different characters in four playlets within the play, which concerns colonels from the four Allies of the Occupation – British, French, American and Russian.

'You think so, Ronnie? Well, you're right, you would be excellent. Pity, because I'm going to play it myself!'

Who could blame him? But I was nevertheless bitterly disappointed. In the event, I was cast as the Russian colonel. The play was directed by the Associate Director, John Gordon Ash, because Frank had so much to do on-stage that he couldn't direct as well. Rehearsals went smoothly and at dress-rehearsal, Peter Ustinov himself arrived, to see his own play performed by the Playhouse company and to attend the Guild meeting after the first night for the usual discussion and dissection of the play that always took place. These sometimes could be embarrassing and tedious affairs, but this occasion was scintillating, due almost solely to Ustinov's wit and dry humour.

As the Russian colonel, I had to sit in a stage-box with the other three, watching the playlets until it was my turn to do my bit, so I was on-stage watching every bit of the action. I would especially watch Frank with a good deal of envy. During the course of the American colonel's playlet, set in a New York bar, Frank as the wicked fairy became a gangster and a fight ensued. On the Monday of the second week, the cufflink on the American colonel's sleeve caught Frank in the eye, scratching his eyeball severely. It swelled up and although Frank struggled on and finished the show, he was to all intents and purposes blind in one eye. A rehearsal call was posted for eleven the following morning.

We all gathered on the stage next day and waited, sipping coffee and waiting for Frank to appear. He did so, his eye bandaged and painful.

'I can't possibly play tonight, the show will have to be cancelled.'

I heard myself saying, 'I'll play it, Frank.'

Frank looked at me, as best he could. 'Do you know it? Could you do it?'

'I've been watching it for a week. I'm sure I know it.'

Frank replied knowingly, 'Yes, I bet you do,' remembering how much I had wanted to play it all along. 'All right. You're on tonight. And I shall be keeping an eye on you.'

'Just the one,' I replied, a wave of excitement and panic descending on me.

John Gordon Ash, the Director, was to take my role and it was announced that the company would meet at five o'clock for a full dress-rehearsal. Therein lay the biggest problem. The costumes. I was at this time almost twice as big as Frank Shelley. I seemed to spend most of the day having fittings, or rather ill-fittings, the wardrobe people searching high and low for bits of material they could let in to enlarge the costumes. The old Russian peasant's costume proved impossible, so I wore a black waistcoat inside which, to make the sleeves of the blouse, I wore a pair of the dresser's mother-in-law's Directoire bloomers – one knicker leg on each arm. 'It's a long time since any man's had both hands inside my mother-in-law's knickers,' she said.

Five o'clock arrived, and the dress-rehearsal with all the quick changes and the props. It took two hours and I coped reasonably well. As we finished, they called the half-hour and at 7.30 I was on.

I have never spent such an exhilarating night in the theatre. The adrenalin was flowing so freely that I sailed through without a prompt. And in those days I had never even heard the word adrenalin. But the excitement was so great that afterwards, having spent a wonderful hour in the pub with the company, I went home to get a good and long night's sleep. I never slept a wink. However, by Wednesday I was completely relaxed. Roll on Saturday night, I thought, what a wonderful audience it will be!

Come Saturday, Frank said, 'My eye's fine now. I think I'll do Saturday.'

You can't always be the cat that gets the cream, I said to myself, but as an underdog you certainly had your day. And if you think the animal metaphors mixed and inept, not so. On Saturday it rained cats and dogs and hardly anybody turned up.

15

A change was about to occur at the Playhouse in the summer of 1954, which some say was to put an end to the Oxford Playhouse company and to true repertory in Oxford. Whether the end would have come in any case, despite this change, is difficult to say.

The change was that the company, meaning the limited company, was bought out by, amalgamated with, taken over by, The London Mask Theatre Ltd, an organisation run by a man called Thane Parker with the Director, Hugh Goldie. Another of their companies was called The Young Elizabethan Theatre Company, and it was the nucleus of actors from this, plus Derek Francis and myself, who made up the new Playhouse Company. All the other actors were given notice. Donald and Christine had already left some months before. Derek, the man of a thousand faces, and I were there, I think, to represent the Old Guard, so that the changeover did not seem so abrupt to the Oxford audiences.

It was, naturally, Frank Shelley who told us of the change, the new management. He called us together at the beginning of the rehearsals for *The Dover Road*. The company always rehearsed in the set of the play that was running at the time, which always looked so very different in the cold light of morning with just a few working lights instead of the glamorous moody lighting it was bathed in for the evening performance. He told us the news in his clearest and most vibrant baritone, and explained that this meant he would be leaving the Playhouse. It was a sad time for him and for all the regulars on the staff, not least of all me. I had grown very fond of Frank, his idiosyncrasies, his eccentricity, his humour and love of life.

'I wish the new company every success,' he boomed, rattling the crystal drops on the vases decorating the set mantelpiece, 'but I shall be surprised if repertory as such can run much longer in Oxford. The trouble with Oxford is, what with amateur dramatic and operatic companies, and the bloody university,' here his voice increased several hundred decibels on the expletive, rattling the plates on the Welsh dresser, 'there are far too many EFFING AMATEURS.' He did not use the word that begins with 'f', he actually said 'effing', but the volume was enough to cause every single leaf of a rubber plant on the table behind the sofa to fall off. There was also a sort of whimpering in the circle, followed by the crash of the exit door. I found out later that Miss Bevis had been coaxed out of her office by the magnetic boom of Frank's voice and she had entered the circle in time for the big 'eff' and had staggered, fainting, out again.

Before Frank started rehearsing what was to be his last play, he gave everyone a fortnight's notice, with the exception of Derek and me, who had to report to Mr Thane Parker's office. I was given a two pounds a week rise, and two weeks later was introduced to the new company.

A lot of splendid talent had arrived: Hugh Manning, Tony Church, Heather Chasen, all to become well-known. Frank Windsor, to become part of the most famous British double-act on television with Stratford Johns as Watt and Barlow in *Z-Cars*. And last, but not by a thousand miles least, Michael Bates. What a funny man. What a delight. The first play we did, *Carrington VC*, centred on a court martial. He played the very dramatic leading role perfectly. The second play, Gogol's *The Government Inspector*, was hilarious. Michael Bates played the lead in that too and was screamingly funny. I played his old servant and thoroughly enjoyed myself.

But more important, this play was another of those milestones in my career that I can look back on and pinpoint. There are several such times that in retrospect are seen to be vital to any success I have achieved. This turning point was the arrival of a young director who had had a successful first play in London and now wanted to work in repertory for a few months to gain experience. His name is Peter Hall, or rather was Peter Hall and is now Sir Peter Hall. We got on very well from the first, he allowing me to put a few extra quips into *The Government Inspector* (it was his own adaptation) and laughing at them more loudly than anyone else during the performance. He was younger than me: about twenty-one, I think. By this time I was almost twenty-five and felt quite an old hand with nearly six years and over a hundred plays under my belt.

In the autumn, Peter decided that we should do some melodrama and old-time music-hall. I was delighted at this news, having immensely enjoyed the ones we did at Aylesbury years ago. The first half of the evening's entertainment was the melodrama, *A London Actress*, in which I played the villain, Moses Mendoza, a man of a certain obvious religious persuasion. A money-lender, a Shylock, a swine and a snake in the grass. I was hissed from start to finish and relished every minute of it. The second half was the Old-Time Music-Hall, in which everyone sang a comic song and I was chosen as the Chairman, with a foaming pint of ale at my elbow, a large gavel in my hand and a joke on my lips. All, of course, appearing to be extempore. Peter himself played the piano and a very accomplished pianist he proved to be. Wearing deathly pale make-up and a drooping moustache, he never smiled once during the evening. A new Assistant Stage Manager, a girl dressed in a pretty frock, stood next to him, simply to turn the pages of the music. She never spoke the whole evening. Her name was Eileen Atkins.

Peter and I both agreed that I should have ready a few replies and snappy ripostes to the audience's barracking which he assured me would inevitably assail the Chairman. Oxford being full of undergraduates of the brighter sort, he said, there was bound to be a wealth of wit flying across the footlights. He had seen it while up at Cambridge (but a matter of two or three years ago!).

So I set to, searching my brain and other people's by way of old copies of *Punch* and the like, for a handful of neat back-answers to compete with the young intelligentsia who would invade the auditorium come next Monday night.

In the event, I found it most difficult to use any of these gems because the great thing about a comic line is that it must be preceded by the right feed line. One or two generalisations such as 'Pour that gentleman back into the bottle,' could be used almost any time, but the more specific heckles could only be answered off the top of the head. The marvellous thing about being the one on stage as opposed to the one in the audience is that the audience is on your side, and will laugh first and think about it later whenever you make any sort of reply, witty or not. In re-introducing an actress who had already done one number, I said, 'And now a lady whom I'm sure you would like to see more of.'

(*Whistles and cheers.*)

Voice from audience: 'Jane Russell.'

(*Laughter.*)

Me: 'You've got a point there, sir.'

(*Laughter.*)

Me: 'In fact you've got two points.'

(*Laughter, applause.*)

Me: 'Now, where were we? Oh yes. There was a rustle in the bushes . . .'

(*Cheers, more applause.*)

Etc. Etc. Not the world's most scintillating or witty exchange, we must all admit. But because the audience knew it was new, fresh that night, for their ears only, they loved it. A trick I learned, and have recognised in other performers since I discovered it, is to pretend you didn't quite hear the remark from the audience and ask them to repeat it. It means that all the audience get to hear it properly, but mainly it gives the performer time to think of an answer.

Voice from audience: 'Mr Chairman!'

Me: 'Sir?'

Voice: 'What would the Lord Chamberlain say about that naked light on the stage?' (referring to the lit candle on the piano.)

Me: (*Brain racing.*) 'I beg your pardon, sir?'

Voice: 'What would the Lord Chamberlain say about that naked light on the stage?'

(*Laughter. More time to think.*)

Me: 'That is not naked, sir, it is fully covered by our insurance policy.'

(*Laughter, applause.* Got away with it again.)

One didn't always get away with it. One night a crowd

of varsity rugby players were in. These heroes of the campus's sole aim at college was to win a blue or a half-blue at the sport, a much-prized award. After one of my replies to a heckler, a cry came from where the rugby lads were sitting.

'Mr Chairman, if they gave out blues for wit, you would be a half-blue.' Clever and unanswerable.

My stock phrase then was always, 'Fifteen love,' and then, 'New balls, please.' It was better than nothing.

Although I've never been a stand-up comedian, I found the Chairman taught me a lot when talking to TV audiences before a show and the like. I shall always look back upon that production with great affection.

A few more shows – including *Saloon Bar* in which I drank real beer on the first night and by the third act wasn't sober enough to quite remember all my lines – and suddenly it was Christmas. You know how it happens, one minute it's August Bank Holiday and the next minute there are twenty-nine shopping days to Christmas. My last show at the Playhouse, indeed my very last show in repertory, was the premiere of a Christmas production called *Listen to the Wind*. This delightful children's musical was written by Angela Jeans and Vivian Ellis and directed by Peter Hall.

For some time I had had the feeling that I was getting deeper and deeper into a very comfortable rut. Living at home, the lovely Jean my constant companion, very popular with the audiences, doing work that was very fulfilling. Nevertheless, big fish in small ponds stagnate. I had to move on. But where and how? The question was answered by my old dear friend and mentor, Glenn Melvyn.

In the three years since I had left Bramhall, he had written a play, a Northern comedy called *The Love Match*, sold it as an idea to Arthur Askey, played a wonderful supporting role he had written for himself and was at that time at the Palace Theatre in London, where the play was in its second year. Now he had written a sequel and wrote to me asking if I would like to appear in its try-out tour. Not only that but as Arthur Askey was not doing the tour, Glenn was playing the lead and he wanted me to play his (Glenn's) part on tour. This involved learning how to stutter. Glenn did the most wonderful stutter and I learned from him, which stood me in great stead for the television series *Open All Hours*, some eighteen or so years later. To put the gilt on the gingerbread, the icing on the cake, he said there was a small part that Jean, my (still unofficial) fiancée, could play. Of course, I accepted like a shot, and so did she. So, for those two reasons, the rut and the offer, this was to be my last show at the Playhouse, as the tour started in January.

Another bonus soon manifested itself and made this step forward not entirely a haphazard journey into the unknown, not entirely a leap into who knows what. In the pub one night after the show, Peter Hall told me he had been asked to direct a production at the Arts Theatre in London called *Mourning Becomes Electra*, Eugene O'Neill's colossal trilogy of plays. He said there were two good parts in it for me, and rehearsals would start in June. Did that fit in with my plans? Not half it didn't; Glenn's play finished in May. I told Peter this.

'Do you have plans after that?' he said.

'Yes,' I replied, 'my plans are to be in *Mourning Becomes Electra* at the Arts Theatre.'

'Splendid,' he said, and splendid it was too. It was what I had dreamed of, being in a play in London.

We had a few half-pints that night, Peter and I. He became slightly morose in his cups and suddenly said, 'You and I will never really get on in this business, Ron.

You have to be queer to get on in this business.' Surprising how quaint that remark seems in these enlightened days. Even reading it as I write it, it seems archaic. In any event, I think I can say without conceit that we both proved him wrong on that score.

The part I was to play in *Listen to the Wind* was that of the gipsy man who appeared only in Act One, but who had a very showy solo number, a song with a mad gipsy-type Spanish dance, not dissimilar to my cavorting in the *Cinderella* panto a couple of years back. It was a part I was to recreate at the Arts Theatre in London the following year, whilst appearing in the third act of another play at the Apollo, both in the same evening. But that is another story.

Back in Oxford in December 1954, the first night arrived, all went well and it got excellent reviews from London as well as local critics. The London crowd all had their eye on Peter as the new Boy Wonder, so they tended to visit us quite often. Maggie Smith, by now an ASM, was in the cast and by now associated much more with the company in general. Through her I renewed my acquaintance with her twin brothers, Alistair and Ian, who had been at my school and also at the architectural college where I had spent five wasted months before deciding that architecture wasn't for me.

I think my reason for leaving was actually the fact that these twins were so brilliant. In a competitive profession like that, I wouldn't be able to make my mark. So of course I had instead chosen the most overcrowded profession of them all. Even in those days, you were lucky to work twenty weeks a year. Yet still the drama schools and children's stage schools continued to churn out the young hopefuls.

There were three young hopefuls in the cast of this

Christmas show. Three very young hopefuls, almost children, playing the leading parts. I'm often amazed at the professionalism of some of these youngsters. They always know their lines, they do exactly as directed and are in every way most reliable. Each night during my number, these three sat beside me, singing the choruses of the song. One evening, one of the girls suddenly got up in the middle of my dance and walked off the stage. Strange, I thought, as I capered and cavorted about like an idiot. That girl has to sing in harmony with the others in a minute, I thought, jumping on my hat. She hurried back just in time. Not enough time for a pee, I thought as I stamped and crashed my way round the stage, building to the big finish. I left the stage with a final flamboyant 'Olé!' and the children carried on with the scene.

'What did she come off for?' I asked Eileen Atkins on the prompt-book.

'She's ill,' was the reply. 'Poor little bugger threw up into the fire bucket.' The child had then calmly come back on-stage and finished the scene.

'You are what we call a real trouper,' I said to her, and I meant it.

Returning to Maggie Smith's brothers. They, or rather one of them, was to feature in a most bizarre episode towards the end of the run of my last play in Oxford.

There was no stage-door-keeper at the Playhouse. In those days hardly any of the rep companies had one, because somehow there seemed to be no need for one. Visitors to us lowly Thespians were few and far between, apart from our friends who would gather in the greenroom after a show and wait for their particular chum, or simply barge into the dressing-room. Sometimes one of the stage-staff would pop their head round the door and announce that so-and-so was downstairs. Now, I didn't know Alistair and Ian Smith quite well enough for them to come to the dressing-room. That is how Vernon came to be chosen as messenger boy. Vernon was a temporary, part-time stage-hand, and also a part-time drunk. That is to say, he started the evening sober and got steadily drunk during the show. He had only been with us for a few weeks, but had already got full value out of the warning buzzer in the pub which led to my downfall with Jessie Matthews.

It was on the Friday night, prior to the play closing on Saturday, that Vernon put his head round the door, or rather crashed heavily through it, and came to rest with his backside on my dressing-table and his hands in my powder-bowl.

'Bugger,' he said, managing to slur even that short sharp expletive. He looked at me through bloodshot eyes.

'Is that what you came to tell me, Vernon?' I enquired.

'I've just washed that,' he said, staring at his white floury hand.

'What did you want?' I persevered.

'I shall smell like a bloody hairdresser,' he replied. 'Alastair Sim to see you downstairs.'

This showed how drunk he was. 'Alistair Smith,' I said. 'You mean Alistair Smith.'

'Thassit. Alistair Smi–(hic) Smith. Upstairs.'

'Downstairs,' I corrected him.

He fully agreed. 'Dhicownsticairs.'

'Goodnight, Vernon.'

'G'night. See you inner pub?'

'You can't even see me now.'

'Asstrue.' And he lumbered out, wiping his powdery hand on the wall as he went.

I wiped off my make-up and dressed. Alistair would wait. I've always hated leaving the theatre or studio without properly cleaning off the grease paint. It makes your eyes sore and you feel generally unclean, unable properly to enjoy your après-show drink. So it must have been ten minutes or so before I trotted downstairs to the green-room, a fairly dark and dingy place, half-full of cast, stage-staff and the odd visitor. There was Alistair Smith, talking to some girl or other.

'Sorry, Alistair, you wanted to see me. Have I kept you waiting?'

He looked puzzled. 'No, I'm just waiting for Maggie.'

I stood rather nonplussed, as Alistair turned away to continue chatting to the girl. Then out of the shadows glided a cloaked figure in a black wide-brimmed hat, looking not unlike the Sandeman's Port advert, except for the hollow eyes, pale complexion and rather sinister smile.

'Good evening, Mr Barker. My name is Alastair Sim.'

It was really he. The drunken Vernon had been right after all, but too drunk to know he was right.

I was, of course, astounded.

'I'm so very sorry to have kept you waiting, Mr Sim,' I managed to mumble. He ignored this.

'I saw the show tonight. I thought you were very good. I'd like you to take the part of the innkeeper in a play I'm doing with George Cole. I start in February. Will that be all right?' The sinister smile had become charming.

Of course, I couldn't do it. Glenn's play was agreed, contracted. The room was now hushed, everyone having recognised perhaps our greatest film comedian, which made it all the more difficult for me to tell him I couldn't be in his play. I stumbled through the explanation as well as I could.

'What a pity,' he said, 'it's a good part. Well, congratulations again on tonight's performance. Goodnight.'

I managed to stammer, 'Perhaps I could offer you a . . .'

'Thank you, no. I have a car waiting.' And he glided away into the night like some benign Phantom of the Opera. The whole room erupted the second he had gone, but I hardly heard it. I was in a rosy daze, once again immeasurably star-struck.

16

I was back home in my little room in Cowley. I had finished the last show at the Playhouse, and was soon to leave for London where we were to rehearse Glenn's play, ready to go on the try-out tour. I had made my farewells to the Playhouse staff and to the other actors, and would never again perform on those beloved boards.

It had been, I realised, just over six years since my first hesitant steps onto the stage at Aylesbury, when I had rushed on in the scene-change and literally struck the matches. I remembered those first exhausting days carting props, making props, on fourpence a week. I remembered the girl students: my darling Janie who took my virginity, and my even more darling Juliet, who caught us at it and was afterwards such a dear sweet companion in those early days. I remembered the misery and desperation of the mime tour. The cold, the penury, the long walk home. I remembered so many things, so vividly. But most of all, I remembered the laughs. God, what laughs I had shared with so many folk in those six terrific years. With Glenn and with Robin, with Frank Shelley, Derek Francis, Johnny Randall. With Donald – so many barely controlled fits of giggles with Donald Hewlett! Big Annie and the sofa spring; what a girl she was.

Dancing in the Moonlight

But now they would remain for ever only memories. I was leaving repertory for good. I was leaving home, and dear old Oxford, for ever. No more of that. I was heading for London to seek my fortune. I was heading for the big time.